Problem S for Fluency and Beyond

Grade One

Maggie Day
Catherine Fosnot

New Perspectives on Learning
Taking the Standards of Practice Seriously

New Perspectives on Learning, LLC
New London CT and Vero Beach FL

ISBN-13: 978-1-7342166-9-1

Table of Contents

Unit Overview

Number Strings versus Number Talks: What is the Difference?

Before you start working with this unit, it is important to understand how strings are crafted and implemented. Many people use the terms "number talks" and "number strings" interchangeably as if they are the same thing. They are not. There are definite similarities because both invite students to think, to share their reasoning, and to discuss and compare the variety of strategies that their peers offer. Discussions like these are critical to a thinking classroom (Liljedahl, 2021). **But talking alone is not sufficient to ensure equity and access.** The crafting of the string, the numbers we use, as well as the juxtaposition of them in the string are all critical to ensure not only engagement but the needed supports to ensure access and equity, and the construction of big ideas. The string is crafted to generate generalization and algebraic thinking, not just a sharing of a variety of computation strategies.

Settle in a comfortable place. Grab a cup of coffee (or another beverage of your choice) and scan the QR code below. If you prefer to use your computer, go to your browser and type in the url:
https://vimeo.com/885366802/f2c5187775

There you will be able to watch a video presentation where more details of the differences between number talks and number strings are described. In the video you will also see strings in action from several classrooms across the grades.

* * * * *

This unit is the seventh book on minilessons using strings of related problems in the *new* full core CFLM series, which is sold only by New Perspectives on Learning. The first book in the series provided number strings for early number sense, addition, and subtraction, whereas the second extended the focus of the use of these two operations to greater amounts. Book three provided 80-100 minilessons using strings for early multiplication and division. The fourth book extended these two operations to greater amounts. The fifth book provided strings for operating with fractions, decimals, and percentages. The sixth, *From Fives and Tens to Automaticity* written for kindergarten, returned the focus to the early years for a much-needed addition to the series. In contrast to the first five, it provided a developmental progression of strings of related problems using the 5-bead rekenrek to build a foundation for prioritizing 5, and the eventual using of the 10-bead rekenrek to develop fluency with addition and subtraction and automaticity of the basic facts up to 10. It is an important precursor for working with the 20-bead rekenrek, which is the beginning point of the rekenrek work in the original first book in the series.

The seventh unit, the one you are holding in your hands, is written for Grade One. It also emphasizes development and automaticity of the basic facts, this time the basic facts to 20. However, it also goes beyond the number and operation work to include strings on algebraic reasoning, geometry, measurement, and data. For that reason, in this book we refer to strings as "problem strings"—a more generic term—in contrast to our earlier terminology of "number strings."

* * * * *

The rekenrek (developed by Adri Treffers at the Freudenthal Institute) is a manipulative that makes use of children's early ability to subitize ones, twos, and threes. As far as we know this ability is most likely innate: research with infants shows they can recognize three sounds as different from two sounds, and three dots as different than two dots (Dehaene and Changeux, 1993). Babies will also look for missing objects if they are shown 3 being put into a box, and then only find 2 when the box is opened (Wynn, 1992). These abilities occur in the first year of life, well before children can count. [Note: Interestingly, Roman Numerals make use of subitizing—i , ii, iii are the symbols used for 1, 2, and 3. Five and ten required two new symbols: v and x. The five and ten are also prioritized—vi is 6, vii is 7, and viii is 8. Nine is represented as ix (1 before 10) and 11 is represented as xi (1 after 10); 15 is xv and 16 is xvi.]

When the rekenrek was first introduced to the U.S. market (Fosnot and Dolk, 2001), there were few resources available for teachers on how to use it and it could only be purchased in The Netherlands. That is now not the case. Today, many publishers carry resources full of activities with the rekenrek, and some companies have even copyrighted their own versions of the rack. Sadly, many of the versions on the market show an ignorance of the research. Some publishers have even translated the Dutch term "*rekenrek*" as "a counting frame." The rekenrek is NOT a counting frame. In fact, it is designed to encourage children to abandon counting strategies in favor of the use of subitizable units and the prioritizing of fives and tens. The translation should be "calculating rack."

Most of the activity books on the market also offer teachers little in the way of understanding a developmental sequence of what to do with the rack. Isolated activities with the rack, even when strung together into sequences and used every day, will not likely produce the intended results of fluency unless they are based on developmental progressions. Teachers are left wondering when to introduce symbols, what to do when fives and tens are not being prioritized, how and when to wean children away from the rack, and how to use it to develop, eventually, automatization of the basic facts. The primary purpose of this newer series (K-5, one unit for each grade) is to provide answers to those questions.

Automatizing the Basic Facts: A Developmental Progression

Section A: Operations and Algebraic Thinking within 10

Reviewing the 10-bead rack. All work with the rekenrek should always begin with ensuring that children can prioritize 5. If they don't understand that there are 5 red beads and 5 white beads within a row on the rack and use this information to group and regroup amounts, they will resort to counting every single bead. The beads shown in the picture are out of play. This is the home position. When doing strings, you will be moving the beads in the problem from the home position to the left, so children can read them left to right, like text. For example, to make a 6 you will slide 6 beads (5 red and 1 white) left. This is the "in play" position. Prioritizing the 5 and 10 is the goal with the rack. For this reason, it is **VERY IMPORTANT** to hold the rack so that as children look at the beads in play, they see the red beads first. Do not vary how you hold the rack—the red beads must always come first, and children should read the rack from left to right. Examples of quick images to use to support prioritizing the 5 (seeing it within greater amounts) can be found in Section A. Keep working with strings of images like these until the numbers 6, 7, 8, 9, and 10 can easily be identified as follows, with no counting needed: 6=5+1; 7=5+2; 8=5+3; 9=5+4 or as 10-1; and 10=5+5. It is **NOT** important to skip count by twos on the rack, or to make the quantities in a variety of ways. Teachers often ask too many times, "Did anyone do it a different way?" If you do this, children will try to please you and come up with all different ways to show the number. It's fine to accept a few ways if children offer them, and it is particularly helpful if you have some children who don't yet conserve the quantity. But, do stay focused on your purpose—prioritizing the 5-structure. The reason this is important will become apparent as you start working on the facts that make ten and as you work on doubles and near doubles with the 20-bead rack to build a foundation for automaticity of the basic facts to 20, a year-end-objective in grade two.

Introducing symbols. As your children become more and more familiar with the above relationships and the 10-bead rack and are confident that the whole has not changed no matter how you move the beads, begin to introduce symbols. As your students share what they have seen and justify the sum, move the beads to represent their strategy, but also write the equation on the side. For example, if a child says, "I just know five plus two is seven," write, "5+2 = 7." But if a child says, "It was six before when you showed five plus one and I know a bead just moved over. Now it's five plus two, so now it is seven." Show the movement of the additional bead and then write, "5 + (1+1) = (5+1) + 1." Children usually do not have trouble with this representation if you move the bead simultaneously to show the action. The symbolic representation records the nesting of 6 inside 7 (the big idea of hierarchical inclusion) and the compensation (+1 -1 to maintain equivalence) and in general the associativity involved. But don't try to introduce the formal terminology of the associative property! For young children, formal language is not the point—developing an understanding of number as rearrangeable quantities that don't change the sum quantity is the point.

Part/whole relations: partial envisioning. As children become more and more familiar with the number relations within the 10-structure, and the symbols, and trust there are 10 and only 10 beads on the rack, you can begin to wean them off the rack by doing partial envisioning—showing one subitizable amount on one side, with the missing addend on the other side, hidden. Start by showing one addend and writing it. Ask, "How many are hiding?" and write, for example, "5 + ? = 8." When children share strategies, uncover the hidden amount and if appropriate move the beads to represent the strategy and then write the missing addend (3) in place of the question mark. You can also introduce subtraction this way. You can say, "We had 8, but I took some away. How many did I take away and hide?" Then write, "8–3 = 5."

Bridging to automaticity: full envisioning. Once students understand the part/whole relations of 10, and partial envisioning is no longer a challenge, it is time to use only symbols. Strings of related problems are presented crafted to generate discussions on the properties of the operations: commutativity, compensation and associativity, and part/whole relations. These are all big ideas for young children. For each problem ask your students to envision the rack in their mind as they think about an answer, but don't show the rack. As students share ask them to defend their answer by explaining what the problem would look like on the rack. Represent what they say on the rack, invite discussion, and then write the equation. It is fine to write the sum on the right of the equal sign, but don't always do that. It is important to develop a strong sense of equivalence and the idea that expressions can be treated as related objects, in contrast to procedures. So, don't hold back with writing equations like the following: 8+2 = 9+1, or 6+4 = 5+5. Eventually, you may not need to invite envisioning. At this point, the rack becomes only a "fall back"—brought out only when students are challenged, or when an answer needs to be checked. At this point, the rack is no longer being used as a manipulative or a model of a strategy; it has become a mental tool for thinking.

In Kindergarten many of your students hopefully used the 5 and 10 racks and already have the facts to 10 automatized. Section A provides strings with the 10-bead rack if you find this is not the case, or if your students need more work to automatize the facts within 10. If your students have already automatized the basic facts within 10, you can skip Section A and start your work on grade one with Section B.

Section B: Operations and Algebraic Thinking within 20

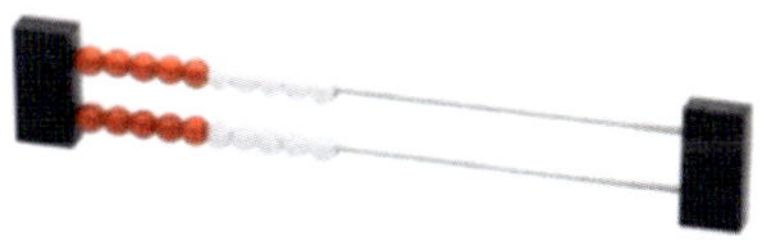

As you work with the 20-bead rack start by reminding students about what they know about fives and tens. Show the rack and ask what they see and how many beads they think there are. This gives you a chance to see if they can prioritize and use the fives and tens as groups. Many will likely say they see 4 groups of fives, or 2 rows of 10. Others will say there are 10 red beads and 10 white beads. Using fives and tens flexibly is critical to getting the basic facts to 20 automatized. The first set of strings, in Section B of this unit, focuses on equivalence and prioritizing 10. Ten can be seen on the 20-bead rack as one complete row, or by 10 red beads. Thus, teen numbers can each be represented as a complete row of ten and more on the bottom (for example 10 on the top and 3 on the bottom or reversed) or as an equivalent expression 5 + 8 (shown as 5 red on the top and 8 on the bottom). Some students will make use of the red beads and immediately see 5 + 8 as equal to 10 + 3. Others may choose to fill the 8 to make a 10 and remove 2 from the 5. Strategies like the latter also lead to compensation (lose 2/gain 2) and associativity. Commutativity is developed by reversing the placement of the beads from top to bottom on the rack. Many children call this, "the turn around." Doubles are easily learned by prioritizing the 10, for example if one envisions 6 as 5 red beads and 1 white bead, 6 + 6 is immediately seen as 10 reds + 2 whites. A near double like 6 + 7 is just one more than 6 + 6 or one fewer than 7 + 7. On the rack, 7 + 7 = 10 + 4 = 14, so the near double is also 10 + 3 or 10 + 5. The equivalent problem of 6 + 8 is also 14 because 1 from the 8 was moved to the 6 using compensation. Building relationships between the facts supports the development of number sense as well as the properties of the operations.

From the Basic Facts to Computational Fluency

Section C: Addition and Subtraction to 100

For the sum of numbers greater than 20, you will need a different model. Different models have different assets and drawbacks. Although connecting cubes can be used to model quantities, they cause children to count all, or to count on, instead of developing other more powerful mental arithmetic strategies. The bead string with alternating groups of 5 red and 5 white cubes might cause children to regroup fives into tens because of the colors, but research in The Netherlands caused the Dutch to abandon this model long ago in favor of the open number line. The bead string with discrete separate beads is a cardinal model just like connecting cubes and researchers found that cardinal models could produce errors in subtraction with confusion about where to start the count when counting backwards. This did not occur when a measurement model of number was developed, and an open number line was used. [Note: The CFLM unit *Measuring for the Art Show* is a great sequence to use to develop a measurement model and the open number line. Use it in the spring of grade one before you begin strings to 100 and then you can use the open number line as a powerful representational tool to represent student strategies during discussions.] A real number line with all the ticks is not a good model because children just count the ticks (turning it into a cardinal model) and then make mistakes about where to start the count. It produces the same confusion that the bead string produces. Many teachers often like to use a hundred bead mathrack or a hundred chart. But these have problems, too. They are also cardinal representations of groups of ten, and the arrangements of the decades one under another makes the distance between some numbers greater, for example 10 is on the right and 11 is way over on the left of the next line. For all these reasons we believe it is best to use the open number line when developing fluency to 100. The open number line can also be extended to a double number line, with one expression on the top and another on the bottom as shown on the cover. This model is a powerful representation of magnitude, equivalence, part/whole relations, and equations.

Start your work with Magnitude and Equivalence, introducing the symbols <, >, and =. The first 10 strings, in Section C, are provided for this work. Then begin working on strategies. The most important strategies for fluency in addition are: 1) splitting both numbers using expanded notation to make partial sums with the tens and ones, for example 32 + 48 = 30 + 40 + 2 + 8 = 70 + 10; 2) keeping one addend whole and adding jumps of tens to it and adjusting, for example 32 + 48 = 32 + 50 – 2; and 3) compensation and associativity to move to a landmark, for example 32 + 48 = (30 + 2) + 48 = 30 + (2 + 48) = 30 + 50.

The most important strategies for subtraction are: 1) jumps of tens back and adjusting, for example 62 – 28 = 62 – 30 + 2, or 62 – 28 = 62 – 20 – 8; and 2) constant difference, for example sliding the difference forward or backward on the number line keeping the distance constant: 62 – 28 = 64 - 30. The algorithms are not required until grade 4. Fluency using place value and properties of the operations is the goal.

The last part of Section C is on figuring out mystery numbers. This section includes strings for part/whole relations, specifically the connection between addition and subtraction, missing addends, subtrahends, and minuends, and in general working on equations.

Beyond Arithmetic: Exploring Space and Shapes

Section D: Geometry

Current research in cognitive development (Spelke, Lee, and Izard, 2011) suggests that babies have two core cognitive systems: one that guides them as they move and another for the analysis and recognition of shapes. But neither system by itself is sufficient to explain the development of the fundamental Euclidean relationships such as length, angle, and direction, which will be needed for higher level understandings of geometry. The two core geometries must be coordinated. Navigational pathways of straight distances and turns that enclose space become understood as line segments and angles that can be used as properties to describe, name, and categorize 2- and 3-dimensional shapes. *Baby's Wild Adventure* and *Shaping Up the Yard* are two CFLM units that support the development and coordination of the two core geometries. But minilessons can also be used to do so. This unit provides many strings of related problems for the development of geometry.

The first part of Section D begins with strings based on navigation and mapping. The problems are given as pathways travelled (for example, 3 straights and 3 turns to get back to the starting point). Students are asked to draw the pathways and determine the shape created. The second part of Section D is full of strings using quick images of 2-dimensional shapes. Students are shown a shape briefly and then asked what shape they saw and how they know. The third and last part of Section D provides strings of problems that involve students in composing and decomposing, first 2-dimensional shapes using pattern blocks, and then quick images of the faces and nets of 3-dimensional shapes to determine the overall shape (platonic solids and prisms).

Section E: Linear Measurement, Data, and Time

In the early years, children usually begin categorizing and labeling lengths and distances traveled with discrete terms. They talk about heights as tall or short and distances and time periods as long or short. Comparative terms come later as children begin to compare relations with seriations (ordering with a continuum). You will hear their language shift to "longer" than the others, or "shorter" than this one, but "longer" than that one. Forman and Hill describe this big idea as comparative variations. Following this ability is the development of the logic of transitivity—if the orange rod is longer than the blue, and the blue rod is longer than the red, then the orange must also be longer than the red. Once these ideas are constructed, the idea of measuring 2 lengths with a third object, such as non-standard units, emerges. And then, eventually, the need for a standard unit develops.

In grade one, the units designed to develop this trajectory are: *Farms and Fences, Measuring for the Art Show, Comparing Favorite Collections,* and *The Timekeepers.* Strings can also be very useful. You will find many in Section E.

References and Resources

Dehaene, S., & Changeux, J.P. (1993). Development of elementary numerical abilities: A neuronal model. Journal of Cognitive Neuroscience, 5, 390–407.

Forman, G. and Hill, F. (1984). Constructive Play. Addison-Wesley.

Fosnot, C.T. and Dolk, M (2001). Young Mathematicians at Work: Constructing Early Number Sense, Addition, and Subtraction. Portsmouth, NH: Heinemann.

Liljedahl, P. (2021). Building Thinking Classrooms in Mathematics, Grades K-12, Thousand Oaks, CA: Corwin.

Wynn, K. (1992). Addition and subtraction by human infants. Nature, 358, 749–750.

Automatizing the Basic Facts

A Developmental Progression

Section A: Operations and Algebraic Thinking

A1: Reviewing the 10-bead Rack (quick images to prioritize 5)

Materials Needed
 Strings A1-A18 require a class-size 10-bead Mathrack™

Show one expression at a time for a few seconds on the rack (not using symbols) and then remove it from view. With these quick images you will only be asking children about the beads they see on their left and how they determined their answer. You will not be using symbols. The string starts with 10. Move all ten beads from the home place on the right to the in-play position on the left (child's viewpoint). Ask, "How many beads do you see and how do you know?" After sufficient discussion on the first problem, move all the beads back to home (the right side), and then move all the red beads back to the left. The second problem supports the use of 5. Again ask, "How many beads do you see now, and how do you know?"

The purpose of this string is to encourage children to see other amounts in relation to 5 and 10. It's possible as you work through the string that students will use the beads remaining on the right (still at home) to determine what is on the left (in play) and this is fine if they do. For example, many children noting just 1 bead on the right often know that 9 beads must be on the left, as 9 is 1 less than 10. Celebrate moments like this but also ensure that everyone understands that you are only asking about how many there are on their left. Point to the ones you mean. As strategies are shared, move the beads on the class-size 10-bead Mathrack™ to represent student thinking. If children start counting from 1, ask them if they know how many red beads there are and encourage them to use what they know. For example, when looking at an image of 6, they should see 5 red and 1 white. Ask how many reds there are. If they know five and don't have to count, ask, "How much is 5 and 1 more?"

A Picture of the Rack from the Child's Viewpoint Showing 10 in play, on the left

The String
10 on the left
5 on the left
7 on the left
6 on the left
9 on the left
8 on the left

Inside One Classroom: A Portion of the A1 Minilesson

Anna (the teacher): Here is our first one. It is going by quickly so make sure you are looking! (*Shows all 10 on the left.*) Ok, thumbs up when you are ready to share how many beads you saw. (*When most thumbs are up, Anna starts discussion.*)

Jodi: Ten! I know because I know 5 + 5 = 10.

Anna: (*Using the Mathrack™*) Like this? You saw 5 red beads and 5 white beads? (*Anna separates the two groups at first with her fingers, moving them apart, and then back together again to show 5 + 5 = 10 so other children can check.*) Wonderful! That was a fast way! Who else just knew 5+5? (*Several hands go up.*) Did anyone do it a different way? Elsa?

Elsa: I knew 5, then I counted on, 6, 7, 8, 9, 10.

Anna: Ok, so this next one will probably be easy then. *(Anna moves the white beads in a group to the right, leaving only the red on the left for a few seconds and then covering the image.)* Ok, what did you see and how do you know? Wow! That was fast! Lots of hands up. Esteban?

Esteban: Five. All the red ones.

Anna: Ok, I knew that would be easy. Everybody knows there are 5 red beads, right? It's great when you use something you know. Then you don't have to count! Here's the next one then (*adds 2 white beads to make it 7)*. Don't forget to show me with a thumb when you are ready. (*Noticing that several students are counting, Anna decides to have pair talk.*) Turn and talk to your elbow partner. I see lots of counting. Talk to a partner about whether counting is needed. Is there a way to just know this one without counting? *(After a few minutes, she resumes whole-group discussion.*) Did anyone have an interesting partner who tried a really fast way?

Maya: (*Counting on to check what her partner has said.*) Hannah said it was like the last time... 5 red beads, but with 2 more white beads, 5+2. I checked, and it is. See... this is 5, so 6, 7.

Anna: Wow! So, if we use 5, a group we know, we can do bigger amounts easily, without counting? We'll name this after you, Hannah. What shall we call it? How about, "Look for 5 and use it?"

Author's notes

The string starts with two "helpers." Counting should not be needed for these. Anna quickly accepts a few strategies and moves on. Knowing where the challenges will be helps her decide when to quickly move on, and when to slow down and promote discussion.

Anna provides discussion here—right where it is needed.

This is also a nice moment to label the strategy to promote ownership of ideas. Doing so values the student who thought of it, and it helps others to think about using it.

A2: Reviewing the 10-bead Rack (quick images to prioritize 5)

This string is very similar to A1. The numbers have only been changed for variety. Show one expression at a time for a few seconds on the rack (not using symbols) and focus children on what they see on the left. Ask students how they determined their answer. As strategies are shared, move the beads on the class-size 10-bead Mathrack™ to represent student thinking.

The String

5 on the left
8 on the left
7 on the left
6 on the left
9 on the left
10 on the left

A3: Reviewing the 10-bead Rack (quick images to prioritize 5)

This string is also very similar to A1. Show one expression at a time for a few seconds on the rack (not using symbols) and then remove it from view.

The String

5 on the left
4 on the left
6 on the left
8 on the left
7 on the left
9 on the left

Behind the Numbers

Note how the strings thus far make use of the structure of the rack? Being able to image how a number 1-10 is related to 5 or to 10 is critical for getting the basic facts automatic. Counting all and counting on strategies for addition are tedious and not sufficient for automaticity. Prior work with the 5-rack was done in kindergarten (see the K unit in CFLM *From Fives and Tens to Automaticity*) so that children would start prioritizing it. The colors of the beads and the grouping of them support children to use five. If some of your children are still counting every bead and not prioritizing the 5, you may need to do more work with them in small groups to encourage the prioritizing of 5. A few more strings like A1 are provided below in case you need more.

A4: Reviewing the 10-bead Rack (quick images to prioritize 5)

This string is like A1.

The String

5 on the left

4 on the left

9 on the left

8 on the left

7 on the left

6 on the left

A5: Reviewing the 10-bead Rack (quick images to prioritize 5)

This string is like A1.

The String

5 on the left

10 on the left

6 on the left

7 on the left

9 on the left

8 on the left

A6: Reviewing the 10-bead Rack (quick images to prioritize 5)

This string is like A1.

The String

2 on the left

7 on the left

3 on the left

8 on the left

9 on the left

A7: Reviewing the 10-bead Rack (quick images to prioritize 5)

This string is like A1.

The String

10 on the left

9 on the left

8 on the left

7 on the left

6 on the left

A8: Reviewing the 10-bead Rack (quick images to prioritize 5)

This string is like A1.

The String

6 on the left

7 on the left

9 on the left

10 on the right

8 on the left

A9: Reviewing the 10-bead Rack (quick images to prioritize 5)

This string is a variation on the prior strings. It introduces missing addends to support algebraic thinking, and it is also working on getting some facts automatic. Prioritizing 5 and the part/whole relations within 5 are still the focus and no symbols are used yet. Use the class-size 10-bead Mathrack™ to create one quick image at a time using the string of problems below, asking students to determine how many more beads are needed. As strategies are shared for determining the answer, move the beads to represent students' thinking. Clear the rack to home each time between problems and then start by letting your students see you moving all 5 red beads to the left.

The String

5 red beads shown on the left, say, "I'm thinking of 8, what should I do to this to make it 8?"

5 red beads shown on the left, say, "I'm thinking of 6, what should I do to this to make it 6?"

5 red beads shown on the left, say, "I'm thinking of 7, what should I do to this to make it 7?"

5 red beads shown on the left, say, "I'm thinking of 9, what should I do to this to make it 9?"

5 red beads shown on the left, say, "I'm thinking of 10, what should I do to this to make it 10?"

5 red beads shown on the left, say, "I'm thinking of 4, what should I do to this to make it 4?"

A10: Reviewing the 10-bead Rack (quick images to prioritize 5)

This string is a variation on A9. It introduces subtraction.

The String

5 red beads shown on the left, say, "I'm thinking of 3, what should I do to this to make 3?"
5 red beads shown on the left, say, "I'm thinking of 8, what should I do to this to make 8?"
5 red beads shown on the left, say, "I'm thinking of 2, what should I do to this to make it 2?"
5 red beads shown on the left, say, "I'm thinking of 7, what should I do to this to make it 7?"
5 red beads shown on the left, say, "I'm thinking of 1, what should I do to this to make it 1?"
5 red beads shown on the left, say, "I'm thinking of 9, what should I do?"

Inside One Classroom: A Portion of the A9 Minilesson

Anna (the teacher): Here is our first one. (*Shows 5 red beads on the left, with the remaining 5 white beads hidden under a cloth.)* I'm thinking of 8. What should I do to make this into 8? How many more do I need to make 8, and how do you know? Thumbs up when you are ready to share. (*When most thumbs are up, Anna starts discussion.)*

Ella: I know because... 1 more is 6. I just remember that one. And 1 more is 7, then 8. *(Holds 3 fingers up showing that she said 3 numbers.)*

Anna: (*Using the Mathrack™ Anna removes the cloth, shows the beads hidden in it, and moves 3 white beads over one-at-a-time to make 8.*) Ella did it by counting on and keeping track. Did anyone do it a different way? Rafael?

Rafael: I started with 10—five red and five white, and then I took 2 away. I knew that would make 8. See? Ella is right. It is 3.

Anna: Jake?

Jake: (Holds up 2 hands, and points to his thumbs.) I agree with Rafael. See, ...5 and 5, but then if I push the thumbs down, I have 4 and 4.

Anna: Hmmm...that's some nice thinking. So, 10 – 2 equals 8. Great. But I already have 5 here, not 4. How many beads do I need, and will they be red or white?

Author's notes

The Mathrack™ is a helpful tool for thinking. Anna uses it here as a representational tool to illustrate the relations under discussion. Note how she supports Jake to imagine the rack instead of his fingers. It is prioritizing the five as an image that is critical at this point. Later in the year, Anna will turn the focus to other pairs that make eight.

A11: Reviewing the 10-bead Rack (quick images to prioritize 5)

Like the string in A9, this string is also designed to support the use of known addition facts by prioritizing the 5 and adding or subtracting some subitizable units as missing addends. Clear the rack each time between problems. Note how the problems in the string are in pairs: -1, +1; -3, +3; and +4, -4.

The String

5 red beads shown on the left, say, “I’m thinking of 4, what should I do to this to make 4?”
5 red beads shown on the left, say, “I’m thinking of 6, what should I do to this to make 6?”
5 red beads shown on the left, say, “I’m thinking of 2, what should I do to this to make it 2?”
5 red beads shown on the left, say, “I’m thinking of 8, what should I do to this to make it 8?”
5 red beads shown on the left, say, “I’m thinking of 9, what should I do?”
5 red beads shown on the left, say, “I’m thinking of 1, what should I do?”

A12: Making ten (equivalence, compensation and associativity, commutativity)

Show one image at a time on the rack in the order below, but with this set of problems ask students how many in all. Record student thinking by both moving beads and then writing numeric symbols after the child shares what she did. For example, if a student says 6 + 4 is the same as 5 + 5, to represent compensation and associativity move one bead over slowly to support children to see the equivalence being discussed, but also write equations as illustrated in the Teacher Note, but on the right of the string (not in it). Lastly, write the answer in the string.

The String

5 + 5
6 + 4
4 + 6
3 + 7
2 + 8

Inside One Classroom: A Portion of the A12 Minilesson

Anna (the teacher): Here is our first one. It is going by quickly, so make sure you are looking! (*Shows 5+5.*) Ok, thumbs up when you are ready to share how many beads you saw. (*Most thumbs go up quickly, so Anna starts discussion.*)

Ilene: I saw 5 and 5. I know it's 10 because all the beads are there and there's 10 beads on the rack.

Anna: Does everyone agree there are 10 beads here? (*There are lots of nods of agreement, so Anna draws a rectangle in the upper left-hand corner of the white board as a text box and writes, 5+5 = 10 inside at the top.*) Let's go on to a second problem then. Here's the next one (*shows 6+4*). Don't forget to show me with a thumb when you are ready.

Esteban: I know it is still 10, because all the beads are still there. You didn't take any away and you can't add any. It has to be 10.

Anna: Wow! That's interesting. Are you saying that 5+5 = 6+4? *(Anna writes the equation.)* Let's all turn and talk about this with a partner. (*After a few minutes Anna resumes a group discussion.)*

Maria: One bead just moved. It's like you took a bead from here and moved it over there. Now there are only 4 here and 6 there because you moved one over.

Anna: One bead just went to the other group? But it is still 10 altogether? Wow, another fast way! (*Using the Mathrack™, Anna shows the image of 6+4 again, then moves a bead from the left to the right, effectively turning 6+4 back into 5+5.)* Let me record that great idea. *(Anna writes, 6+4 = 5+5 as well as, 5 + (1+4) = (5+1) + 4.)* One bead just moved, but we still have 10! How cool is that! This idea saves a lot of counting. We can just imagine beads moving. Ok. Here's the next one *(Anna shows 4+6.)*

Rafael: It's a turn around one.

Anna: So, it's still 10? Hmm... If I flip the rack though it will look different because of the colors are switching places but it is still 4 + 6? Do you think we could find Esteban's idea about beads moving again? Did some beads move? Let's turn and talk about this.

Author's notes

Anna makes sure her students know this is a quick image, reminding them to stay focused on the rack.

Notice how Anna writes the equivalence of the two expressions. Doing so promotes an understanding that the equal sign reflects two expressions being equal. The representation of the 1 moving also represents the associative property in a way that children can understand. At this age it is attributed to the child, though. The formal terminology is not used.

Teacher Note

This string is designed to support the development of some big ideas that will help students to automatize the combinations that make 10: equivalence, compensation and associativity, and commutativity. When a child shares, record the strategy by moving beads first, so other students understand what is being shared. Subsequently, record the strategy using numerals. For example, if a child says, "I used the last problem and just moved a bead over," move the bead over showing how 5+5 became 6+4. Then write, 6+4 = 5+5, as well as 5 + (1+4) = (5+1) + 4. Explain that mathematicians just use parentheses to show their readers how they are thinking about it. In this case, first the 1 was with a 4 to make 5; then, it was moved over to the other 5 to make 6 and now 4 remains. Teachers often shy away from this representation because they think it is too formal for children. But, to children, it makes perfect sense because it represents exactly what was said. So, don't be shy about it! Once strategies are shared and represented and there is consensus about the sum, underneath 5+5=10 write 6+4=10. Note how the representation of just the string is kept clean? This should not be erased. Erase only the representation of the thinking when more space is needed as you go on with the string, keeping the string clean with the derived sums only, visible, and intact. This allows students to easily see relations in the sums as well. If a child uses commutativity and says 4+6 = 6+4, write an equation to show the equivalence. Don't just write the answer.

A13: Making ten (equivalence, compensation and associativity, commutativity)

This minilesson is like A12. Show one image at a time on the class-size 10-bead Mathrack™ in the order below and invite students to share what they saw and how many beads there are in all. Record student thinking by both moving beads and writing numeric symbols as strategies are shared. When recording, emphasize equivalence by writing equations.

The String

9 + 1

8 + 2

7 + 3

6 + 4

4 + 6

5 + 5

A14: Making ten (equivalence, compensation and associativity, commutativity)

This minilesson is like A12. Show one image at a time on the class-size 10-bead Mathrack™ in the order below and invite students to share what they saw and how many beads there are in all. Record student thinking by both moving beads and writing numeric symbols as strategies are shared. When recording, emphasize equivalence by writing equations.

The String

9 + 1

7 + 3

8 + 2

5 + 5

4 + 6

A15: Making ten (equivalence, compensation and associativity, commutativity)

This minilesson is like A12. Show one image at a time on the class-size 10-bead Mathrack™ in the order below and invite students to share what they saw and how many beads there are in all. Record student thinking by both moving beads and writing numeric symbols as strategies are shared. When recording, emphasize equivalence by writing equations.

The String

5 + 5

4 + 6

8 + 2

5 + 5

4 + 6

A16: Making ten (equivalence, compensation and associativity, commutativity)

This minilesson is like A12.

The String

5 + 5

4 + 6

9 + 1

8 + 2

7 + 3

A17: Making ten (equivalence, compensation and associativity, commutativity)

This minilesson is like A12.

The String

5 + 5
4 + 6
3 + 7
7 + 3
8 + 2

A18: Making ten (equivalence, compensation and associativity, commutativity)

This minilesson is like A12.

The String

4 + 6
3 + 7
5 + 5
7 + 3
8 + 2

A19: Partial envisioning (part/whole, commutativity)

Materials Needed

Strings A19-A35 require a class-size 10-bead Mathrack™ and a cloth for partial envisioning.

As your children become more and more familiar with the pairs that make ten, continue to wean them off the rack by doing partial envisioning—showing one amount on one side, with the addend on the other side hidden. This also supports algebraic thinking. Start by showing one addend and writing it, for example, "5 + ? = 10." Ask, "How many are hiding?" When children share strategies, uncover the hidden amount and if appropriate move the beads to represent the strategy and then write the missing addend in place of the question mark. In this case it is 5. You can also introduce subtraction this way. You can say, "We had 10, but I took some away. How many did I take away and hide?" When students share, write, "10 – 5 = 5."

Show one image at a time in the order below, each time saying how many beads are shown and writing the number shown, followed by a question mark, an equal sign, and the result, as shown below. Ask students to think about the rack and the beads hidden. Ask them what number would replace the question mark. As students share, ask for justifications, and once consensus is reached, erase the question mark, and replace with the missing addend.

The String	Write:
5 (red) shown on the left, 5 (white) hidden	5 + ? = 10
6 shown, 4 hidden	6 + ? = 10
4 shown, 6 hidden	4 + ? = 10
3 shown, 7 hidden	3 + ? = 10
7 shown, 3 hidden	7 + ? = 10

A20: Partial envisioning (part/whole and commutativity)

Show one image at a time in the order below, each time asking, "What number goes where the question mark is? Imagine the rack. How many beads are hidden?" This string is like A19.

The String	Write:
6 shown on the left, 4 hidden on the right	6 + ? = 10
4 shown on the left, 6 hidden on the right	4 + ? = 10
9 shown, 1 hidden	9 + ? = 10
1 shown, 9 hidden	1 + ? = 10
2 shown, 8 hidden	2 + ? = 10
8 shown, 2 hidden	8 + ? = 10

A21: Partial envisioning (part/whole and commutativity)

Show one image at a time in the order below, each time asking, "What number goes where the question mark is? Imagine the rack. How many beads are hidden?" This string is like A19.

The String	Write:
9 shown on the left, 1 hidden on the right	9 + ? = 10
1 shown, 9 hidden	1 + ? = 10
2 shown, 8 hidden	2 + ? = 10
8 shown, 2 hidden	8 + ? = 10
3 shown, 7 hidden	3 + ? = 10
7 shown, 3 hidden	7 + ? = 10

A22: Partial envisioning (part/whole and commutativity)

Show one image at a time in the order below, each time asking, "What number goes where the question mark is? Imagine the rack. How many beads are hidden?" This string is like A19.

The String	Write:
6 shown on the left, 4 hidden on the right	6 + ? = 10
4 shown on the left, 6 hidden on the right	4 + ? = 10
7 shown, 3 hidden	7 + ? = 10
3 shown, 7 hidden	3 + ? = 10
8 shown, 2 hidden	8 + ? = 10
2 shown, 8 hidden	2 + ? = 10

A23: Partial envisioning (part/whole and commutativity)

Show one image at a time in the order below, each time asking, "What number goes where the question mark is? Imagine the rack. How many beads are hidden?" This string is like A19.

The String	Write:
8 shown on the left, 2 hidden on the right	8 + ? = 10
2 shown on the left, 8 hidden on the right	2 + ? = 10
9 shown, 1 hidden	9 + ? = 10
1 shown, 9 hidden	1 + ? = 10
7 shown, 3 hidden	7 + ? = 10
3 shown, 7 hidden	3 + ? = 10

A24: Partial envisioning (part/whole and subtraction)

Show one image at a time in the order below, each time asking, "What number goes where the question mark is? Imagine the rack. There are 10 beads on the rack. How many beads did I take away and hide?" This string is like A19 *but note that it introduces subtraction.*

The String	Write:
6 shown on the left, 4 hidden on the right	10 - ? = 6
4 shown on the left, 6 hidden on the right	10 - ? = 4
9 shown, 1 hidden	10 - ? = 9
1 shown, 9 hidden	10 - ? = 1
2 shown, 8 hidden	10 - ? = 8

A25: Partial envisioning (part/whole and subtraction)

Show one image at a time in the order below, each time asking, "What number goes where the question mark is? Imagine the rack. How many beads did I take away and hide?" This string is like A24.

The String	Write:
4 shown on the left, 6 hidden on the right	10 - ? = 4
6 shown, 4 hidden	10 - ? = 6
9 shown, 1 hidden	10 - ? = 9
1 shown, 9 hidden	10 - ? = 1
8 shown, 2 hidden	10 - ? = 8

A26: Partial envisioning (part/whole, commutativity)

Show one image at a time in the order below, each time asking, "What number goes where the question mark is? Imagine the rack. How many beads are hidden?" This string is like A19 but note that *the position of the missing addend is different. Also note the shift of positions in the last problem.*

The String	Write:
9 hidden on the left, 1 (white) shown on the right	? + 1 = 10
1 hidden on the left, 9 shown on the right	? + 9 = 10
2 hidden on the left, 8 shown on the right	? + 8 = 10
8 hidden on the left, 2 shown on the right	? + 2 = 10
8 **shown** on the left, 2 **hidden** on the right	8 + ? = 10

A27: Partial envisioning (part/whole, commutativity)

This string is like A26.

The String	Write:
1 hidden on the left, 9 shown on the right	? + 9 = 10
9 hidden on the left, 1 (white) shown on the right	? + 1 = 10
2 hidden on the left, 8 shown on the right	? + 8 = 10
8 **shown** on the left, 2 **hidden** on the right	8 + ? = 10
7 **shown** on the left, 3 **hidden** on the right	7 + ? = 10
7 hidden on the left, 3 shown on the right	? + 3 = 10

A28: Partial envisioning (part/whole, commutativity)

Show one image at a time in the order below, each time asking, "What number goes where the question mark is? Imagine the rack. How many beads are hidden?" This string is like A26.

The String	Write:
8 **shown** on the left, 2 **hidden** on the right	8 + ? = 10
7 **shown** on the left, 3 **hidden** on the right	7 + ? = 10
7 hidden on the left, 3 shown on the right	? + 3 = 10
1 hidden on the left, 9 shown on the right	? + 9 = 10
9 hidden on the left, 1 (white) shown on the right	? + 1 = 10
2 hidden on the left, 8 shown on the right	? + 8 = 10

A29: Partial envisioning (part/whole, compensation, and associativity)

This string is like A19 in terms of the directions. Note, however, that the string is designed to promote a conversation on compensation and associativity.

The String	Write:
5 (red) shown on the left, 5 (white) hidden	5 + ? = 10
6 shown on the left, 4 hidden	6 + ? = 10
7 shown on the left, 3 hidden	7 + ? = 10
8 shown, 2 hidden	8 + ? = 10
9 shown, 1 hidden	9 + ? = 10

A30: Partial envisioning (part/whole, compensation, and associativity)

This string is like A29. It is also designed to promote a conversation on compensation and associativity. As you record, think about how you might represent the compensation and associativity with parentheses. For example, when discussing the relationship between the first two problems, if a child says, "2 red beads moved over to the white beads," to record the thinking you might write, (3+2) + 5 = 3 + (2+5). Then erase the question mark and write, 3 + 7 = 10. This representation shows both the thinking and the result.

The String	Write:
5 (red) shown on the left, 5 (white) hidden	5 + ? = 10
3 shown, 7 hidden	3 + ? = 10
2 shown, 8 hidden	2 + ? = 10
1 shown, 9 hidden	1 + ? = 10
4 shown, 6 hidden	4 + ? = 10

A31: Partial envisioning (part/whole, compensation, and associativity)

This string is like A30. It is also designed to promote a conversation on compensation and associativity. As you record what children say, represent the compensation and associativity with parentheses where appropriate.

The String	Write:
5 (red) shown on the left, 5 (white) hidden	5 + ? = 10
4 shown, 6 hidden	4 + ? = 10
3 shown, 7 hidden	3 + ? = 10
2 shown, 8 hidden	2 + ? = 10
1 shown, 9 hidden	1 + ? = 10

A32: Partial envisioning (part/whole, compensation, and associativity)

This string is like A30. Note though that the position of the missing addend varies.

The String	Write:
5 (red) shown on the left, 5 (white) hidden	5 + ? = 10
6 shown, 4 hidden	6 + ? = 10
7 hidden, 3 shown	? + 3 = 10
2 hidden, 8 shown	? + 8 = 10
1 hidden, 9 shown	? + 9 = 10

A33: Partial envisioning (part/whole, compensation, and associativity)

This string is designed to help children focus on the relationship between what is being removed and the resulting difference. If the minuend stays the same, as the subtrahend increases, the difference decreases. Show one image at a time in the order below, each time asking, "What number goes where the question mark is? Imagine the rack. How many beads did I take away and hide?"

The String	Write:
10 shown on the left, 0 hidden on the right (under a cloth)	10 - ? = 10
9 shown on the left, 1 hidden on the right	10 - ? = 9
8 shown on the left, 2 hidden on the right	10 - ? = 8
7 shown on the left, 3 hidden on the right	10 - ? = 7
6 shown on the left, 4 hidden on the right	10 - ? = 6
5 shown on the left, 5 hidden on the right	10 - ? = 5

A34: Partial envisioning (part/whole, compensation, and associativity)

This string is like A33. Show one image at a time in the order below, each time asking, "What number goes where the question mark is? Imagine the rack. How many beads did I take away and hide?"

The String	Write:
5 shown on the left, 5 hidden on the right	10 - ? = 5
4 shown on the left, 6 hidden on the right	10 - ? = 4
3 shown on the left, 7 hidden on the right	10 - ? = 3
2 shown on the left, 8 hidden on the right	10 - ? = 2
1 shown on the left, 9 hidden on the right	10 - ? = 1
0 shown on the left, 10 hidden on the right	10 - ? = 0

A35: Partial envisioning (part/whole, compensation, and associativity)

This string is like A33. But here, the subtrahend is increasing by 2.

The String	Write:
9 shown on the left, 1 hidden on the right	10 - ? = 9
7 shown on the left, 3 hidden on the right	10 - ? = 7
5 shown on the left, 5 hidden on the right	10 - ? = 5
3 shown on the left, 7 hidden on the right	10 - ? = 3
1 shown on the left, 9 hidden on the right	10 - ? = 1

A36: Full envisioning (equivalence, compensation, and associativity)

Materials Needed

Strings A36-A47 require a class-size 10-bead Mathrack™ only when needed.

With this next set of strings, you will only write the problems symbolically, one problem at a time. Encourage children to envision the rack, to picture it in their minds. Only use the rack as a "fall back" when children are challenged, to represent a strategy under discussion, or to check answers when there are disagreements. In this set of strings, you'll want to encourage children to look in the string for other problems that might be helpful. The purpose of doing so is to encourage children to make use of the big ideas they have been constructing without needing to depend on the rack. When recording, emphasize equivalence by writing equations. Represent the compensation and associativity with parentheses and the commutativity with the two expressions as described in the Teacher Note on page 20 and the dialogue box on page 19. It's possible at this point that many of your students will just know some of the facts. If so, then only the sum needs to be written.

The String

5 + 5
6 + 4
7 + 3
8 + 2
9 + 1

A37: Full envisioning (equivalence, compensation, and associativity)

This string is like A36. When recording, emphasize equivalence by writing equations. Represent the compensation and associativity with parentheses and the commutativity with the two expressions as described in the Overview. It's possible at this point that many of your students will just know some of the facts and then only the sum needs to be written.

The String

10 + 0
9 + 1
8 + 2
5 + 5
4 + 6
3 + 7

A38: Full envisioning (equivalence, compensation, and associativity)

This string is like A36.

The String

9 + 1

7 + 3

5 + 5

6 + 4

8 + 2

A39: Full envisioning (equivalence, compensation, and associativity)

This string is like A36.

The String

8 + 2

9 + 1

5 + 5

6 + 4

7 + 3

A40: Full envisioning (equivalence and commutativity)

This string is like A36 but note that it is crafted to support the use of commutativity.

The String

8 + 2

2 + 8

1 + 9

9 + 1

5 + 5

6 + 4

A41: Full envisioning (equivalence and commutativity)

This string is like A40.

The String

7 + 3

3 + 7

4 + 6

6 + 4

5 + 5

A42: Full envisioning (equivalence and commutativity)

This string is like A40.

The String

9 + 1

1 + 9

2 + 8

8 + 2

7 + 3

3 + 7

A43: Full envisioning (equivalence and commutativity)

This string is like A40. With the last two problems, notice whether students count on from the first addend. If they do, facilitate discussion on whether it might be easier to think of the last problem as 9 + 1 (or 6 + 4 for the prior problem).

The String

2 + 8

8 + 2

7 + 3

3 + 7

4 + 6

1 + 9

A44: Full envisioning (part/whole)

This string is designed to support children to understand the relationship of subtraction to addition.

The String

2 + 8

10 - 8

10 - 2

3 + 7

10 - 3

10 - 7

A45: Full envisioning (part/whole)

This string is like A44. It is designed to support children to come to understand the relationship of subtraction to addition.

The String

10 - 3

10 - 7

3 + 7

2 + 8

10 - 8

10 – 2

A46: Full envisioning (part/whole)

This string is like A44. It is designed to support children to come to understand the relationship of subtraction to addition.

The String

10 – 2

2 + 8

10 - 8

10 - 7

3 + 7

10 – 1

9 + 1

A47: Full envisioning (part/whole)

This string is like A44. It is designed to support children to come to understand the relationship of subtraction to addition.

The String

10 – 1

9 + 1

10 – 2

2 + 8

6 + 4

10 - 4

10 - 6

Section B: Operations and Algebraic Thinking within 20

B1: Equivalence, Prioritizing 10

Materials Needed

Strings B1-B27 require a class-size 20-bead Mathrack™

With this next set of strings, you will be using the 20-bead rack. It is helpful to introduce the 20-bead rack with the storybook and the CFLM unit *The Double Decker Bus.* If you do not have the book or unit, you can just show students the rack and allow them to determine how many beads there are on it. Make sure that the red beads are always shown first – on the students' left. Support them to make use of the groups of 5 and 10 instead of counting every bead.

This string supports the understanding of equivalence and the prioritizing of ten. Show the images long enough to allow children to see the groups of five but not long enough to count each bead separately. Invite a few children to share their answers with the whole group. Then show the image again to check their solutions. Record student thinking symbolically, such as: 10 = 7 + 3 and as 6 + 4 = 7 + 3. Emphasize how the equal sign means the two expressions are equivalent. Too often we write the answer only on the right of the equal sign only and then children develop the misconception that the equal sign means the answer is coming. Some even come to believe that the two representations above are written wrong! Emphasize the equivalence!

The String

10 on the top, all beads on the bottom are out of play
5 on the top, 5 on the bottom
6 on the top, 5 on the bottom
6 on the top, 4 on the bottom
8 on the top, 2 on the bottom
7 on the top, 5 on the bottom

Inside One Classroom: A Portion of the B1 Minilesson

Anna (the teacher): Here is our first one. *(Shows briefly only the top row, and all hands go up.)* Wow! Everyone's hand is up. How many? *(A chorus of "ten" is heard.)*

Ok, how about this one? *(Shows briefly 5 red beads on the top, and 5 red on the bottom.)* What do you see? How do you know? Thumbs up when you are ready to share. *(When most thumbs are up, Anna starts discussion.)*

Sonia: I know... 10! Because there are 5 on the top and 5 on the bottom. There are no white ones, so I know there are 5 on the top and 5 on the bottom. And 5 and 5 are 10.

Anna: Wow! Sonia was able to just see the fives without counting each bead! That's really helpful! Okay, here's the next one. *(Shows briefly 6 on the top and 5 on the bottom.)* What do you see? How do you know? Thumbs up when you are ready to share... Nicholas?

Nicholas: I started with 10—five red on the top and five red on the bottom. Then I saw there was one more white, on the top. I know that would make 11...

Anna: Pedro?

Pedro: *(Holds up six fingers.)* I agree with Nicholas See, the 5 was a 5 but then it became a 6. 5 + 5 = 10, so I know 6 + 5 is 11.

Anna: Hmmm... I like how you used the problem 5 + 5 to figure out 6 + 5. Those 5s are sure handy! You knew a ten was in this number, and 1 more made 11! Okay, ready? Here's the next one.

Author's notes

The 20-bead Mathrack™ is a helpful tool for thinking. Note how Anna uses it here as a representational tool and how the problems in the string are carefully designed to encourage the prioritizing of five and ten.

B2: Equivalence, Prioritizing 10, and Compensation

This string is like B1, but each of the first four problems equals 10 and will likely engender a discussion on compensation.

The String

5 on the top + 5 on the bottom
4 on the top + 6 on the bottom
3 on the top + 7 on the bottom
2 on the top + 8 on the bottom
8 on the top + 5 on the bottom
4 on the top + 7 on the bottom

B3: Equivalence, Prioritizing 10, and Compensation

This string is like B2. The first four problems all have the same answer of 10 again. They can be solved by finding the 5 within the larger number and realizing the remaining beads are also 5. The next two problems can be solved by prioritizing ten as a row of 10 and counting on. In the string, 10 can be seen as a full row, or as 5 red + 5 remaining beads.

The String

9 on the top, 1 on the bottom
8 on the top, 2 on the bottom
7 on the top, 3 on the bottom
4 on the top, 6 on the bottom
10 on the top, 2 on the bottom
3 on the top, 10 on the bottom

B4: Equivalence, Prioritizing 10

This string is like B2 but a little more challenging. Support students to find the ten and use it.

The String

5 on the top, 5 on the bottom
5 on the top, 6 on the bottom
7 on the top, 5 on the bottom
4 on the top, 5 on the bottom
6 on the top, 4 on the bottom
9 on the top, 5 on the bottom
2 on the top, 9 on the bottom
8 on the top, 5 on the bottom

B5: Compensation and Associativity

This string focuses on prioritizing ten and compensation, but it also illustrates what happens when one bead is exchanged for another consistently and supports the generalization of associativity.

The String

10 on the top, 4 on the bottom
9 on the top, 5 on the bottom
8 on the top, 6 on the bottom
7 on the top, 7 on the bottom
6 on the top, 8 on the bottom
5 on the top, 9 on the bottom
7 on the top, 9 on the bottom

Inside One Classroom: A Portion of the B5 Minilesson

Anna (the teacher): Here we go. Everyone ready? *(Briefly shows 10 beads on the top, and 4 red on the bottom.)* What do you see? How do you know? Thumbs up when you are ready to share. *(When most thumbs are up, Anna starts discussion.)*

Alberta: I see 10 on the top – all the red and white beads, that's 10 and 4 red on the bottom. It's easy with a ten. You just add four more. I just know that 10 and 4 are 14.

Anna: Thanks, Alberta. That's great how you focused on the 10 beads at the top and added on the rest. Using 10 is helpful, isn't it? Okay, here's the next one. *(Shows briefly 9 on the top and 5 on the bottom.)* What do you see? How do you know? Thumbs up when you are ready to share... Jose?

Jose: I know...it's the same answer as the one before... 14.

Anna: Esme can you explain why Jose thinks it's the same answer as the problem we just did...10 + 4?

Esme: This problem has 9 beads at the top and 5 beads at the bottom. The other one had 10 beads on the top and 4 beads on the bottom. I think maybe he imagined one bead went to the bottom?

Anna: Interesting...so 9 + 5 is equal to 10 + 4. You said that if you move one bead – taking it away from one number and adding it to another number, it's the same answer? I'm going to write that using parentheses to show what the beads did. First, that one bead was with the 9 to make a ten, so I'm going to write: (9 + 1) + 4, but then a bead on the bottom moved over to be with the 4 to make 5, 9 + (1 + 4). So, (9 + 1) + 4 = 9 + (1 + 4). The parentheses show what is happening with the beads. The 10 lost 1 and the 4 gained 1. Turn and talk about this with an elbow partner. Is this true? Does 10 + 4 = 9 + 5? *(As pair talk ensues, Anna moves around listening in to several of the conversations. Knowing what is being said helps her decide on her next move.)*

Anna: Esme, you and Alberta were having an interesting conversation. Would you explain to the group what you were talking about?

Esme: Alberta said it was like a "give and take" and at first, I didn't understand what she meant. But then I saw it! It is like 10 lost one, and 4 got it!

Author's notes

This string focuses on compensation and associativity. Anna takes this moment to introduce parentheses as a way to show what is happening with the beads - one bead is associated with the number on the top, then it gets removed and another bead associates with the number on the bottom. But the answer stays the same.

Anna's move to pair talk is important here. Note how the dialogue has now shifted to kids talking to kids. It is not about providing answers to the teacher. It is now about sense-making and justifying ideas to each other.

B6: Compensation and Associativity

This string is like B5.

The String

10 on the top + 0 on the bottom
9 on the top + 1 on the bottom
10 on the top + 5 on the bottom
9 on the top + 6 on the bottom
10 on the top + 4 on the bottom
9 on the top + 5 on the bottom
7 on the top + 7 on the bottom

B7: Compensation and Associativity

This string is like B5.

The String

10 on the top, 6 on the bottom
9 on the top, 7 on the bottom
8 on the top, 8 on the bottom
10 on the top, 2 on the bottom
9 on the top, 3 on the bottom
3 on the top, 9 on the bottom
4 on the top, 8 on the bottom

B8: Compensation and Associativity

This string is like B5.

The String

10 on the top, 6 on the bottom
9 on the top, 7 on the bottom
10 on the top, 4 on the bottom
9 on the top, 5 on the bottom
9 on the top, 6 on the bottom
4 on the top, 8 on the bottom
8 on the top, 7 on the bottom

B9: Compensation and Associativity

This string is like B5, with the introduction of commutativity with the last problem.

The String

9 on the top, 9 on the bottom
8 on the top, 10 on the bottom
10 on the top, 6 on the bottom
9 on the top, 7 on the bottom
9 on the top, 5 on the bottom
4 on the top, 10 on the bottom
5 on the top, 9 on the bottom

B10: Compensation and Associativity

This string is like B5. The last problem offers the challenge for students to make a helper (5 + 10).

The String

9 on the top, 5 on the bottom
8 on the top, 6 on the bottom
7 on the top, 7 on the bottom
10 on the top, 4 on the bottom
8 on the top, 10 on the bottom
9 on the top, 9 on the bottom
6 on the top, 9 on the bottom

B11: Compensation, Associativity, and Commutativity

This string focuses on commutativity and associativity. The string asks students to associate two with the eight to make a ten. If one sees the group of 5 red in the 8, then what is left is 3 + 2, two subitizable small groups that make 5. It challenges students to see 8 + 5 = 10 + 3 and 8 + 7 = 10 + 5.

The String

8 on the top, 2 on the bottom
2 on the top, 8 on the bottom
5 on the top, 8 on the bottom
8 on the top, 5 on the bottom
7 on the top, 8 on the bottom
8 on the top, 7 on the bottom

Inside One Classroom: A Portion of the B11 Minilesson

Anna (the teacher): Okay, is everyone ready for the next one? Thumbs up when you are ready to share how many beads you saw. *(Anna is on the third problem and briefly shows 5 beads on the top and 8 beads on the bottom.)*

Riyana: I saw 5 red on the top... 5 red on the bottom...and 3 more. That's two groups of 5 red beads. – that's 10 and 3 more, so it's 13.

Anna: Does everyone agree there are 13 beads here? *(There are several nods of agreement. Molly shoots her hand up.)* Molly – what did you see?

Molly: I saw 13 too... I saw 5 on the top and 8 on the bottom. The last problem, 8 + 2, was 10, so I knew it was a 10 and then there were 3 left over... 13.

Anna: That's fascinating. Are you saying that 8 + 5 = 10 + 3? *(Anna writes the equation on the board.)* Let's all turn and talk about this with a partner. (*After a few minutes Anna resumes a group discussion.)* Who would like to share what your partner was thinking? Ralph?

Ralph: My partner said that Molly made a 10 by giving 8 two more beads. Then she took 2 of the beads from the 5 and imagined they moved to the 8 to make a ten. *(Anna demonstrates this thinking on the rack.)*

Anna: That's so cool! So, by taking 2 beads from the 5 and giving 2 more beads to the 8, we can turn 8 + 5 into 10 + 3? *(Anna moves the two beads back and forth between the rows to demonstrate.)* I'm going to use parentheses to write what the two beads are doing (8 + 2) + 3 = 8 + (2 + 3). Wow! It is helpful to make a 10 when we can, isn't it? Okay, ready for the next one? *(Anna briefly shows 8 beads on the top and 5 on the bottom. Almost everyone's thumb comes up quickly.)* Who would like to share their thinking?

Milo: That's the same as before! You just switched the beads.

Anna: Tell us more...

Milo: Before it was 5 on top and 8 on the bottom. Now it is 8 on the top and 5 on the bottom. It's the switcheroo! You can switch the numbers around but it's still the same answer. (*Anna writes 8 + 5 = 5 + 8 = 13 on the board.)*

Author's notes

Notice how Anna writes the equivalence of the two expressions. Doing so promotes an understanding that the equal sign reflects two things being equal. The use of parentheses and the representation of the 2 moving also represents the associative property in a way that children understand. At this age the idea of give and take is attributed to the child, though. The formal terminology is not needed. To show the commutativity the rack is just flipped. At first, the 8 is on the top, and the 5 is on the bottom. Flipping it causes the 5 to be on the top and the 8 is now on the bottom.

B12: Compensation, Associativity, and Commutativity

This string is like B11.

The String

6 on the top, 5 on the bottom
5 on the top, 6 on the bottom
8 on the top, 7 on the bottom
7 on the top, 8 on the bottom
5 on the top, 9 on the bottom
9 on the top, 5 on the bottom
7 on the top, 7 on the bottom

B13: Compensation, Associativity, and Commutativity

This string is like B11.

The String

9 on the top, 8 on the bottom
8 on the top, 9 on the bottom
6 on the top, 8 on the bottom
8 on the top, 6 on the bottom
5 on the top, 7 on the bottom
7 on the top, 5 on the bottom
6 on the top, 6 on the bottom

B14: Doubles and Near Doubles

This string focuses on doubles and using doubles to calculate the sum of near doubles. Doubles must be automatic to be helpful in solving near doubles. Automaticity with doubles is achieved by prioritizing the ten. For example, on the rack 7 + 7 can be easily seen as 10 red beads and 4 white beads. The last problem is not a double, but 9 + 9 or 8 + 8 might be helpful in solving it. The last problem presents a nice challenge: 7 + 9 = 8 + 8.

The String

5 on the top, 5 on the bottom
6 on the top, 6 on the bottom
7 on the top, 7 on the bottom
8 on the top, 8 on the bottom
9 on the top, 9 on the bottom
8 on the top, 9 on the bottom
7 on the top, 9 on the bottom

B15: Doubles and Near Doubles

This string is like B14.

The String

10 on the top, 2 on the bottom
6 on the top, 6 on the bottom
5 on the top, 5 on the bottom
4 on the top, 4 on the bottom
8 on the top, 8 on the bottom
10 on the top. 6 on the bottom
5 on the top, 5 on the bottom
6 on the top, 6 on the bottom
7 on the top, 7 on the bottom
7 on the top, 8 on the bottom
6 on the top, 8 on the bottom

B16: Compensation, Associativity, Commutativity, Doubles and Near Doubles

This string is like B14.

The String

5 on the top, 5 on the bottom
7 on the top, 7 on the bottom
10 on the top, 10 on the bottom
9 on the top, 9 on the bottom
8 on the top, 8 on the bottom
8 on the top, 7 on the bottom
8 on the top, 6 on the bottom

B17: Doubles and Near Doubles

This string is like B14. It supports students in using doubles to understand near doubles. The double 7 + 7 can help with near doubles 7 + 6 (one less) and 7 + 8 (one more).

The String

5 on the top, 5 on the bottom
5 on the top, 6 on the bottom
5 on the top, 5 on the bottom
5 on the top, 4 on the bottom
7 on the top, 7 on the bottom
7 on the top, 8 on the bottom
6 on the top, 7 on the bottom
6 on the top, 8 on the bottom

B18: Compensation, Associativity, Commutativity, Doubles and Near Doubles

This string is like B14.

The String

5 on the top, 5 on the bottom
4 on the top, 5 on the bottom
7 on the top, 7 on the bottom
7 on the top, 6 on the bottom
8 on the top, 7 on the bottom
8 on the top, 8 on the bottom
7 on the top, 9 on the bottom

B19: Doubles and Near Doubles

This string is like B14.

The String

6 on the top, 6 on the bottom
7 on the top, 6 on the bottom
5 on the top, 6 on the bottom
7 on the top, 5 on the bottom
8 on the top, 8 on the bottom
8 on the top, 9 on the bottom
9 on the top, 9 on the bottom
7 on the top, 9 on the bottom

B20: Doubles and Near Doubles and Compensation

This string starts with doubles and near doubles, but then incorporates compensation to challenge students to see problems that are on either side of a double – where one bead is moved – are equivalent to the double. $7 + 7 = 6 + 8$. $(6 + 1) + 7 = 6 + (1+ 7)$.

The String

8 on the top, 8 on the bottom
7 on the top, 8 on the bottom
9 on the top, 8 on the bottom
7 on the top, 9 on the bottom
7 on the top, 7 on the bottom
7 on the top, 6 on the bottom
8 on the top, 7 on the bottom
6 on the top, 8 on the bottom

B21: Partial envisioning (part/whole)

As your students become more and more familiar with combinations to 20, you can begin to wean them off the rack by doing partial envisioning. For partial envisioning, only one number is shown, and students are asked to consider a second being added or a subtrahend being removed. This practice supports algebraic thinking and introduces subtraction and addition more formally.

These initial strings use the context of the double decker bus to introduce partial envisioning on the 20-bead math rack. Passengers get on (addition) and passengers get off (subtraction). Keeping it in the context can help students with partial envisioning when they begin.

Briefly show the beads for the quick image. Have students determine how many passengers are on the bus. Then say, "___ passengers get on/off." But *do not model* this on the rack. Write the problem symbolically on the board. Give students time to think and share what they think the answer is. Then model their thinking on the math rack and record their answers on the board.

The String	Say:	Write:
3 on the top, 5 on the bottom	"5 get on"	8 + 5 = ?
4 on the top, 10 on the bottom	"5 get off"	14 - 5 = ?
4 on the top, 9 on the bottom	"5 get on"	13 + 5 = ?
8 on the top, 9 on the bottom	"10 get off"	17 - 10 = ?
9 on the top, 6 on the bottom	"10 get off	15 - 10 = ?

B22: Partial envisioning (part/whole)

This string is like B21.

The String	Say:	Write:
5 on the top, 2 on the bottom	"5 get on"	7 + 5 = ?
4 on the top, 10 on the bottom	"5 get off"	14 - 5 = ?
8 on the top, 7 on the bottom	"5 get off"	15 - 5 = ?
4 on the top, 8 on the bottom	"10 get off"	12 - 10 = ?
6 on the top, 3 on the bottom	"10 get on"	9 + 10 = ?

B23: Partial envisioning (part/whole)

This string is like B21.

The String	Say:	Write:
7 on the top, 4 on the bottom	"5 get off"	11 - 5 = ?
4 on the top, 9 on the bottom	"5 get off"	13 - 5 = ?
8 on the top, 7 on the bottom	"5 get on"	15 + 5 = ?
9 on the top, 9 on the bottom	"10 get off"	18 - 10 = ?
2 on the top, 3 on the bottom	"10 get on"	5 + 10 = ?

B24: Partial envisioning (part/whole)

This string builds upon the last set but does not use the support of the bus. After showing the quick image on the rack and asking students to determine the amount of beads, instead of saying passengers get on or off, just write the equation and have students share their answer. You can then model their thinking on the rack. For example, with the first problem, show 2 on the top and 5 on the bottom as a quick image. Ask children what they saw and establish that it is 7. Then write 7 + 8 without moving any beads and without showing the rack. Ask, "How many now?" The addition of 8 can be added in any way students wish. Encourage them to add in places that make the solution easy. Represent their thinking on the math rack.

The String	Write:
5 on the top, 4 on the bottom	9 + 6 = ?
8 on the top, 7 on the bottom	15 - 9 = ?
6 on the top, 10 on the bottom	16 - 7 = ?
2 on the top, 6 on the bottom	8 + 7 = ?
6 on the top, 9 on the bottom	15 - 7 = ?

B25: Partial envisioning (part/whole)

This string is like B24.

The String	Write:
4 on the top, 5 on the bottom	9 + 7 = ?
6 on the top, 10 on the bottom	16 - 9 = ?
10 on the top, 5 on the bottom	15 - 6 = ?
7 on the top, 7 on the bottom	14 - 5 = ?
7 on the top, 6 on the bottom	13 - 8 = ?

B26: Partial envisioning (part/whole)

This string is like B24.

The String	Write:
5 on the top, 5 on the bottom	10 + 6 = ?
6 on the top, 10 on the bottom	16 - 8 = ?
8 on the top, 10 on the bottom	18 - 9 = ?
6 on the top, 8 on the bottom	14 - 7 = ?
2 on the top, 5 on the bottom	7 + 8 = ?

B27: Partial envisioning (part/whole)

This string is like B24.

The String	Write:
3 on the top, 5 on the bottom	8 + 6 = ?
4 on the top, 10 on the bottom	14 - 6 = ?
8 on the top, 8 on the bottom	16 - 9 = ?
8 on the top, 7 on the bottom	15 - 7 = ?
6 on the top, 8 on the bottom	14 - 10 = ?

B28: Partial envisioning (part/whole)

Materials Needed

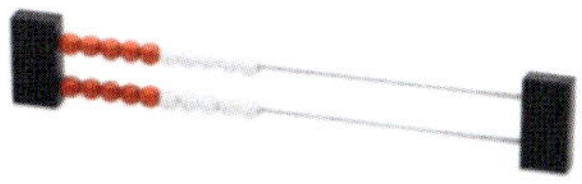

Strings B28-B35 require a class-size 20-bead Mathrack™ and a cloth to cover the beads.

This next set of strings asks students to determine a mystery number. They are asked to figure out what happened when given the initial and final amount. First show a quick image of the beads from the string. Ask students, "How many?" "How do you know?" Have students share how many are on the rack. Then remove beads (behind a cloth so students do not see what you remove) and briefly show a new amount. Ask students, "What do you see now?" Have students determine and share the amount. For example, with the first problem tell students, "We started with 15 and now have 10, what happened?" Write an equation with the missing subtrahend "15 - ? = 10" Ask students what you did and what number goes where the question mark is.

The String	Remove:	Write:
10 on the top, 5 on the bottom	5 from the bottom	15 - ? = 10
10 on the top, 5 on the bottom	5 from the bottom, 1 from the top	15 - ? = 9
9 on the top, 9 on the bottom	9 from the top, 1 from the bottom	18 - ? = 8
10 on the top, 6 on the bottom	9 from the top	16 - ? = 7
9 on the top, 7 on the bottom	6 from the bottom	16 - ? = 10
8 on the top, 4 on the bottom	8 from the top, 2 from the bottom	12 - ? = 2

B29: Partial envisioning (part/whole)

This string is like B28.

The String	Remove:	Write:
7 on the top, 10 on the bottom	9 from the bottom	17 - ? = 8
9 on the top, 8 on the bottom	9 from the bottom, 1 from the top	17 - ? = 7
10 on the top, 4 on the bottom	3 from the top, 4 from the bottom	14 - ? = 7
7 on the top, 7 on the bottom	7 from the top, 2 from the bottom	14 - ? = 5
10 on the top, 6 on the bottom	6 from the bottom, 1 from the top	16 - ? = 9
6 on the top, 8 on the bottom	6 from the top, 1 from the bottom	14 - ? = 7

B30: Partial envisioning (part/whole)

This string is like B28.

The String	Remove:	Write:
6 on the top, 7 on the bottom	5 from the bottom	13 - ? = 8
10 on the top, 5 on the bottom	5 from the bottom, 1 from the top	15 - ? = 9
9 on the top, 9 on the bottom	9 from the top, 1 from the bottom	18 - ? = 8
10 on the top, 6 on the bottom	9 from the top	16 - ? = 7
9 on the top, 7 on the bottom	6 from the bottom	16 - ? = 10
8 on the top, 4 on the bottom	8 from the top, 2 from the bottom	12 - ? = 2

B31: Partial envisioning (part/whole)

This string is like B28.

The String	Remove:	Write:
5 on the top, 6 on the bottom	5 from the top	11 - ? = 6
10 on the top, 1 on the bottom	9 from the top	11 - ? = 9
10 on the top, 2 on the bottom	2 from the top, 2 from the bottom	12 - ? = 8
6 on the top, 6 on the bottom	6 from the top, 1 from the bottom	12 - ? = 5
6 on the top, 7 on the bottom	6 from the top	13 - ? = 7
10 on the top, 3 on the bottom	5 from the top, 3 from the bottom	13 - ? = 5

B32: Partial envisioning (part/whole)

This set of strings also asks students to figure out the mystery number, but this time the mystery number is what you started with—the minuend. The first number given in the string is the difference–what remains after you have taken an amount (the subtrahend) away from the mystery number.

Show the quick image on the 20-bead rack. Have students determine how many there are. Tell them, "This is what is left! I want you to figure out how many I started with." For the first problem, say, 'I took 5 away from my mystery number and this is what is left. Can you figure out what number I started with? What is the mystery number?" Write the equation on the board and ask them to figure out the mystery number. Show their thinking on the math rack. When consensus is reached, record the answer in the string, replacing the ? with the correct minuend. For example, the solution to the first problem is 15 = 20 – 5.

The String	Write:
10 on the top, 5 on the bottom	15 = ? – 5
10 on the top, 4 on the bottom	14 = ? – 6
10 on the top, 4 on the bottom	14 = ? – 1
10 on the top, 4 on the bottom	14 = ? – 5
10 on the top, 3 on the bottom	13 = ? – 5
10 on the top, 3 on the bottom	13 = ? – 6
10 on the top, 5 on the bottom	15 = ? – 7

B33: Partial envisioning (part/whole)

This string is like B32.

The String	Write:
5 on the top, 4 on the bottom	9 = ? – 5
5 on the top, 4 on the bottom	9 = ? – 7
9 on the top, 0 on the bottom	9 = ? – 2
0 on the top, 8 on the bottom	8 = ? – 5
4 on the top, 4 on the bottom	8 = ? – 9
4 on the top, 4 on the bottom	8 = ? – 6
2 on the top, 5 on the bottom	7 = ? – 5

B34: Partial envisioning (part/whole)

This string is like B32.

The String	Write:
5 on the top, 5 on the bottom	10 = ? – 6
5 on the top, 4 on the bottom	9 = ? – 6
5 on the top, 1 on the bottom	6 = ? – 9
3 on the top, 0 on the bottom	3 = ? – 9
5 on the top, 0 on the bottom	5 = ? – 9
5 on the top, 4 on the bottom	9 = ? – 8
2 on the top, 5 on the bottom	7 = ? – 8

B35: Partial envisioning (part/whole)

This string is like B32.

The String	Write:
5 on the top, 5 on the bottom	10 = ? – 3
5 on the top, 1 on the bottom	6 = ? – 7
2 on the top, 0 on the bottom	2 = ? – 9
5 on the top, 1 on the bottom	6 = ? – 5
8 on the top, 0 on the bottom	8 = ? – 5
10 on the top, 3 on the bottom	13 = ? – 5
7 on the top, 6 on the bottom	13 = ? – 7

B36: Full envisioning (Doubles/Near Doubles)

Materials Needed

Strings B36-B53 require a class-size 20-bead Mathrack™ only when needed

Full envisioning is an important step in automatizing the facts to 20. This objective is not required until the end of grade 2, so if all your students don't reach automaticity that is ok. The work you are doing here is only to build a foundation for automaticity. This work continues throughout grade 2. For these strings, you will not be displaying the problems on the rack, only writing the problems on chart paper or the whiteboard. The rack is only used to model strategies if needed, for example if different answers are given and children need the visual support of the model to check solutions during the discussion. Write the problems one at a time on the board, each time giving students time to think and asking them to show when they are finished thinking by giving a thumbs-up. Ask individual children to share their thinking. Represent the thinking with numeric symbols and equations. Use the rack to provide support if needed.

This first section focuses on doubles. Encourage students to make use of the 10 red beads, for example to see 6 + 6 as equal to 10 + 2. The last problem asks students to consider a near double. Some students may use 9 + 9 and remove one; others may use 8 + 8 and add one. Still others may use 10 + 10 and subtract 3.

The String

4 + 4
5 + 5
6 + 6
7 + 7
8 + 8
9 + 9
8 + 9

B37: Full envisioning (Doubles/Near Doubles)

This string uses doubles to support near doubles. 5 + 6 and 5 + 4 are one more (and one less) than the double 5 + 5. 5 + 6 = (5 + 5) + 1 and 5 + 4 = (5 + 5) – 1.

The String

5 + 5
5 + 6
7 + 7
8 + 7
8 + 8
6 + 6
6 + 7

B38: Full envisioning (Doubles/Near Doubles)

This string is like B37.

The String

2 + 2
2 + 3
8 + 8
9 + 8
7 + 8
4 + 4
4 + 5
3 + 5

B39: Full envisioning (Doubles/Near Doubles)

This string uses doubles to support near doubles and compensation. By associating one with a different number, it challenges students to see how these problems are related and have the same answer as the double. For example, 7 + 7 = 6 + 8 can be seen as 7 + (1 + 6) = (7 + 1) + 6.

The String

5 + 5

4 + 6

7 + 7

6 + 8

6 + 6

5 + 7

8 + 8

7 + 9

B40: Full envisioning (Doubles/Near Doubles, Part/Whole)

This string has related addition and subtraction problems to encourage students to use addition to accomplish subtraction. The problems encourage students to consider how doubles and near doubles may be helpful in solving subtraction.

The String

5 + 5

10 - 5

6 + 6

12 – 6

6 + 7

13 – 6

11 – 6

15 – 7

B41: Full envisioning (Doubles/Near Doubles, Part/Whole)

This string is like B40.

The String

7 + 7

14 – 7

8 + 8

16 – 8

7 + 8

15 – 8

15 – 7

B42: Full envisioning (Doubles/Near Doubles, Part/Whole)

This string is like B40.

The String

8 + 8

16 – 7

16 – 9

16 – 10

7 + 10

7 + 9

18 – 9

18 - 10

9 + 9

8 + 7

15 – 7

B43: Full envisioning (compensation, associativity)

This string focuses on compensation, associativity, and prioritizing tens. With 9+8, students will likely be supported to take one from the 9 to make 10+7. Likewise, 8+6 can be seen as 10+4 and 7+5 as 10+2.

The String

10 + 7

8 + 9

6 + 9

8 + 6

8 + 4

8 + 7

7 + 5

B44: Full envisioning (compensation, associativity)

This string is like B43.

The String

10 + 2

9 + 3

9 + 5

8 + 5

8 + 6

8 + 9

7 + 8

B45: Full envisioning (compensation, associativity)

This string is like B43.

The String

10 + 7

8 + 9

6 + 9

8 + 6

8 + 4

8 + 7

7 + 5

B46: Full envisioning (part/whole)

This string incorporates both addition and subtraction problems and encourages students to use addition problems to solve subtraction and use the 5- and 10-structures.

The String

15 – 10

10 + 5

14 – 5

9 + 5

12 - 10

12 – 5

12 - 8

B47: Full envisioning (part/whole)

This string is like B46.

The String

10 + 5

15 – 6

11 – 5

11 – 9

3 + 9

12 – 5

5 + 8

B48: Full envisioning (part/whole)

This string is like B46.

The String

14 – 10

14 – 9

16 – 10

16 – 9

9 + 9

15 – 9

9 + 6

15 – 7

B49: Full envisioning (part/whole)

This string is like B46.

The String

17 – 9

18 – 9

9 + 10

15 – 9

9 + 6

15 – 7

13 - 6

B50: Full envisioning (mystery numbers)

This next set of strings invites students to determine the missing number without the rack. The rack is only used if a student is challenged and needs the tool as support.

The String

13 = ? + 10

13 = ? + 9

13 = ? + 4

12 = ? + 9

12 = ? + 8

11 = ? + 8

B51: Full envisioning (mystery numbers)

This string is like B50.

The String

15 = ? + 10

15 = ? + 9

15 = ? + 8

13 = ? + 8

13 = ? + 5

12 = ? + 7

B52: Full envisioning (mystery numbers)

This string is like B50.

The String

18 = ? + 10

18 = ? + 9

17 = ? + 9

17 = ? + 8

14 = ? + 9

14 = ? + 8

B53: Full envisioning (mystery numbers)

This string is like B50.

The String

10 = ? – 5

9 = ? – 6

8 = ? – 7

10 = ? – 6

9 = ? – 7

9 = ? – 5

From the Basic Facts to Computational Fluency

Section C: Operations and Algebraic Thinking within 100

C1: Magnitude

These number strings focus on magnitude and ask students to think about the placement of numbers on a number line from 1 – 100. In doing so, students must consider numbers as space and distance - how near or far a number is from other numbers and how the measured distances compare.

To begin, draw a line using the meter stick and write 0 and 100 at the end points. Then ask children to close their eyes. While eyes are shut, mark the line for the first number (50), but don't write 50. Only draw the tick. Then ask children to open their eyes and try to guess the number you have marked. As children share their ideas encourage them to share justifications. Doing so supports discussion on number relations. After sufficient discussion use the meter stick to check and mark 50 underneath the tick. Continue with the string doing one number at a time and leaving all agreed upon marks visible as you proceed. This can also be a great time to introduce magnitude signs as students explain where a number might be on the line in relation to another. For example, for the second problem below, after discussion you might write that $75 > 50$ and $75 < 100$.

The String

50

75

25

10

90

60

57

Inside One Classroom: A Portion of the C1 Minilesson

Anna (the teacher): *(Anna draws a line on the board using a meter stick and marks the end points 0 and 100.)* Ready? Ok. Close your eyes while I mark a number. *(Anna measures 50 and places a mark on the middle of the line.)* Ok. Open your eyes. What number do you think this is? How do you know? Show me with your thumbs when you are ready to share.

Jacob: That's 50! It's right in the middle between 0 and 100. 50 + 50 is 100, so that must be 50.

Anna: I see lots of nods. Does everyone agree that is 50? *(There are lots of nods of agreement.)* Okay, let's check. *(Anna measures and marks 50 underneath the tick.)* Ok – get ready for the next one. Close your eyes. *(Anna measures 75 cm and makes another mark where 75 should be.)* Ok, open your eyes and show me with a thumb when you think you know what number this is. Lily?

Lily: I think that is 60.

Anna: Tell me more. Why do you think it is 60?

Lily: I know the mark is more than 50. See it's after the 50.

Anna: So, you said 60 is more than 50. I'm going to record that over here using a new symbol. Mathematicians use this symbol to show how numbers are related. *(Anna writes 60 > 50.)* The arrow always points to the smaller number so this says 60 is greater than 50. That's nice how you are using the 50 that we just marked to figure out that it must be more. Maya what do you think?

Maya: I think it's even more. Look – it's halfway between 50 and 100. 60 would be a lot closer to the 50.

Anna: Does that make sense Lily?

Lily: I think so. 60 is 10 more than 50. The space between the numbers looks more than 10.

Raj: It's halfway between the 50 and the 100.

Anna: That's interesting. How can that help us?

Lily: I know! It reminds me of quarters. Two quarters are 50, one more is 75 and another would be 100. It must be 75.

Anna: Oh, quarters. That is interesting. How did quarters help Lily? Turn and talk.

Author's notes

Notice how Anna pushes Lily to explain her thinking and then goes back to Lily when Maya contributes new thinking.

This string is designed carefully to support students to think about numbers in relation to other numbers. Students need to consider the placement and magnitude of numbers in comparison to those already placed. The 75 is placed in relation to the 50 and the 100. This also provides the teacher with opportunities to write expressions that show inequalities and comparisons of magnitude: 75 > 60 and 75 < 100.

C2: Magnitude

This string is like C1.

The String

50

25

10

40

60

90

15

20

82

C3: Magnitude

This string is like C1.

The String

10

20

80

40

65

70

35

C4: Magnitude

This string is like C1.

The String

5

95

10

15

85

30

45

62

C5: Magnitude and Equivalence

This next set of strings focuses on magnitude and equivalence. Students are asked to compare two sets of numbers and determine whether they are equivalent, and if not, which one is greater. This section reinforces equivalency and the equal sign (=) and reviews the greater than (>) and less than (<) representation. Use the double number line to show student thinking when figuring out each side of the equation.

For each problem in the string, write the problem on the board and ask students if the two amounts are equivalent. Record student thinking as shown below. Cuisenaire rods can be used if needed. (This is like the work done in the CFLM unit *Farms and Fences.*) If the two expressions are not equivalent, have students determine which is greater and record with the appropriate sign.

The String

5 + 5 and 10

5 + 5 and 2 + 5 + 3

10 + 5 and 5 + 5 + 2

10 + 5 and 9 + 6

2 + 5 + 3 + 10 and 10 + 10

5 + 3 + 10 and 8 + 5

Inside One Classroom: A Portion of the C5 Minilesson

Anna (the teacher): *(Anna writes 5 + 5 and 10 with a space in between.)* Are these amounts equal? Show me with your thumbs when you have an idea… Riyana?

Riyana: Yes! 5 + 5 is 10. So…both sides are ten.

Anna: Wiggle your pinkies if you agree with Kelly. *(Almost everyone wiggles their pinkies.)* That was so automatic for you. You know that 5 + 5 is 10. How nice is that! *(Anna smiles and draws the bars to make a double open number line that represents the equivalency of both sides.)*

I'm going to write an equal sign between the two sides. This shows that they are equivalent. (*Anna writes 5 + 5 = 10.)* Okay – here is the next one. *(Anna writes 5 + 5 and 2 + 5 + 3 on the board with space between them.)* What does everyone think? Are these the same? Are they equivalent?... Thumbs up when you are ready… Jose?

Jose: I know that 5 + 5 is 10. Just like before. But I'm not sure. There are more numbers on the other side.

Abby: I think they are the same. There are more numbers – but look, 3 and 2 are 5. So, it's just 5 and 5 again.

Anna: Wow! Turn to a partner and talk about what Abby did. *(Anna draws rods of 3 and 2 under the 5 to make a double number line then adds another rod of 5 to show the equivalence. She then writes 5 + 5 = 3 + 2 + 5.)* Okay I'm going to write another problem. Watch closely! *(Anna writes 10 + 5 and 5 + 5 + 2 with a space in between.)* What do you think? Are these equivalent? Thumbs up when you have an idea.

Ralph: There's the 5 and 5 again. So, both sides have a 10. *(Anna draws bars to represent the rods with two jumps of five above a jump of 10.)* But now one side has a 5 and the other only has a 2. That's not the same. *(Anna adds a jump of 2 onto the fives and a jump of 5 onto the 10.)*

Anna: What numbers shall I mark at the end?

Ralph: That's 12 and 15. 10 + 2 is 12 and 10 + 5 is 15. *(Anna records the totals at the endpoints of the double number line which shows that 15 is greater than 12.)* And 15 is more than 12.

Author's notes

The double number line is an important model which helps students compare both sides of an equation. It can also be a helpful tool when thinking about inequalities and magnitude.

Anna supports pair talk on Abby's strategy at this moment to ensure all students are engaged and discussing Abby's idea. Abby moves around and listens in to see if all understand. Big ideas are at play here—the commutative and associative properties!

Anna: Interesting – I can't put my equal sign here. I need to write a sign that shows 15 is greater than 12. Mathematicians write it this way to show that 15 is greater. *(Anna writes 15 >12 and then also writes 10 + 5 > (5 + 5) + 2. This last representation is important because it shows that adding everything up to get the sum is not always needed. 5 + 5 can be thought of as an interchangeable equivalent object to 10. No addition is even needed to know this is an inequality. One only must compare 5 and 2 to know which expression is greater.)*	Notice how Anna introduces the greater than sign in context - after modeling the difference between 12 and 15 on the double number line Anna then reaffirms students' identities as mathematicians by explaining that this is a sign mathematicians use to record when one amount is greater than another.

C6: Magnitude and Equivalence

This string is like C5 but note that the numbers are getting larger. Therefore, Cuisenaire Rods should no longer be used. It is best here to start recording the numbers as jumps on the open number line. But continue to represent one expression on the top, and one on the bottom. If students are challenged by this representation, you can use the rods as a fall back to support understanding, but you will need to build some of the larger numbers, for example making 20 with 2 tens (2 orange rods).

The String

20 and 10 + 5 + 5

2 + 3 + 10 and 5 + 10 + 5

8 + 2 + 10 and 3 + 5 + 10

8 + 20 and 25 + 3

25 and 15 + 8 + 2

8 + 3 + 10 and 20

C7: Magnitude and Equivalence

This string is like C5. Use a double open number line with jumps in place of the rods to represent the thinking. Remember to record with =, <, or > signs.

The String

6 + 4 and 5 + 5

5 + 10 and 5 + 5 + 5 + 5

10 + 9 and 4 + 1 + 5 + 10

10 + 10 + 10 + 10 and 30

26 + 14 and 30 + 6 + 5

C8: Magnitude and Equivalence

This string is like C5. For the first problem, you can continue to use the double number line, showing how a jump of 24 compares to a jump of 34. Students can also consider how much more 34 is than 24.

The String

34 and 24

20 + 14 and 24 + 10

40 + 34 and 60 + 24

44 + 30 and 64 + 10

70 + 14 and 82 + 10 + 4

C9: Magnitude and Equivalence

This is like string C5.

The String

50 and 50

25 + 25 and 24 + 26

25 + 26 and 25 + 24

30 + 30 and 29 + 32

39 + 44 and 40 + 45

C10: Magnitude and Equivalence

For this next set of strings, students are asked to contemplate if the equations are true or false. If false, students should determine which sign would make it true (=, <, >). Record each equation one at a time on the board. Ask students if the statement is true or false. Have students share their answers and explain their thinking. Record their thinking using a double number line. If they agree it is false, ask them what sign would make it true and record their answer.

The String

25 = 25

10 + 10 + 5 = 5 + 5 + 10

52 < 25

50 + 2 = 49 + 2

10 + 52 = 50 + 2 + 10

20 + 52 > 50 + 20 + 4

C11: Magnitude and Equivalence

This string is like C10.

The String

12 = 21

54 > 45

50 + 4 = 40 + 5

40 + 5 + 10 = 50 + 5

40 + 15 = 49 + 5

20 + 20 + 15 = 40 + 5 + 10

C12: Magnitude and Equivalence

This string is like C10.

The String

40 = 40

40 + 9 = 49 + 10

42 < 24

50 + 20 = 49 + 19 + 2

10 + 19 + 10 = 20 + 29

5 + 20 + 10 = 19 + 11 + 2 + 3

C13: Magnitude and Equivalence

This string is like C10.

The String

39 = 93

$33 > 99$

40 - 1 = 39 + 1

39 + 10 = 30 + 9 + 10

30 + 19 = 49 + 10

49 + 2 + 10 = 50 + 1 + 10

C14: Strategies for Addition to 100 (Splitting)

This string of related problems encourages students to use expanded notation and make partial sums. Sometimes this strategy is termed splitting since the addends are split by column. Splitting is a common strategy that students construct early on. It is based on additive structuring and an emerging recognition of place value. For example, 37 is thought of as 30 + 7. So, 37 + 12 would be 30 + 7 + 10 + 2, and when rearranged by tens and ones becomes 30 + 10 + 7 + 2 = 49. In contrast, later in development, once students have a deeper understanding of place value and have constructed the big ideas of unitizing and place determines value, multiplicative structuring is used and 37 + 12 is thought of as 3 tens + 1 ten + 7 + 2. Both strategies should be recorded on an open number line. While it can be tedious to record all the parts, over time this lends itself to a discussion of how splitting is not always the most efficient strategy as there are so many parts to keep track of!

This string starts off with two problems that can be used to solve the third. The fourth and fifth problems are a pair, but students will need to make the helper problem (30 + 10). This is also the case with the last two problems, students will need to make the helper problems (50 + 10) and (20 + 70).

The String

20 + 20

6 + 3

26 + 23

7 + 2

37 + 12

4 + 6

56 + 14

24 + 77

Inside One Classroom: A Portion of the C14 Minilesson

Anna (the teacher): *So, how about this next one...26 + 23.*

Riley: I used the problems before, 6 + 3 and 20 + 20.

Anna: Tell us more.

Riley: 26 is really 20 and 6 and 23 is 20 and 3. So I added up the 20s like before and got 40. Then I know 6 and 3 are 9. So, 40 + 9 is 49.

Anna: How nice that you were thinking about the problems we already did, and you made connections! *(Anna draws a representation on the open number line.)*

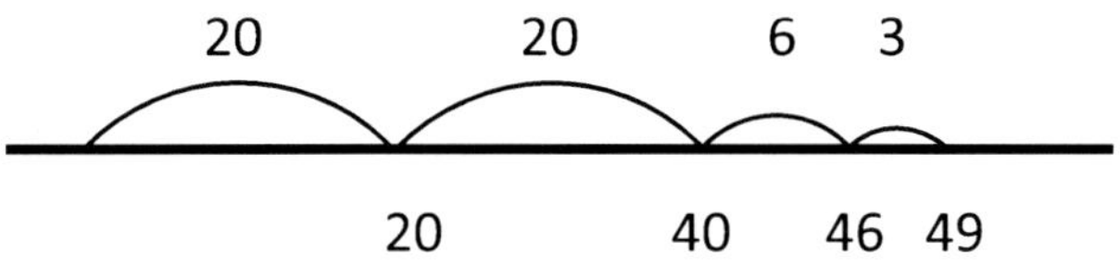

Turn and talk to your neighbor about what Riley noticed. (*Anna moves around and listens into conversations as students talk in pairs. Noting that Rafi has done something similar, but is employing multiplicative structuring, she invites him to share his strategy next.)*

Anna: Rafi, your strategy is sort of like Riley's, but it is a little bit different. Tell us what you did.

Rafi: I knew the 2 was 2 tens. So, I thought of 26 as 2 tens + 6 and 23 as 2 tens + 3. So that was 4 tens + 9 and I knew that was 49.

Anna: *(Anna draws a representation on the open number line to show Rafi's strategy.)*

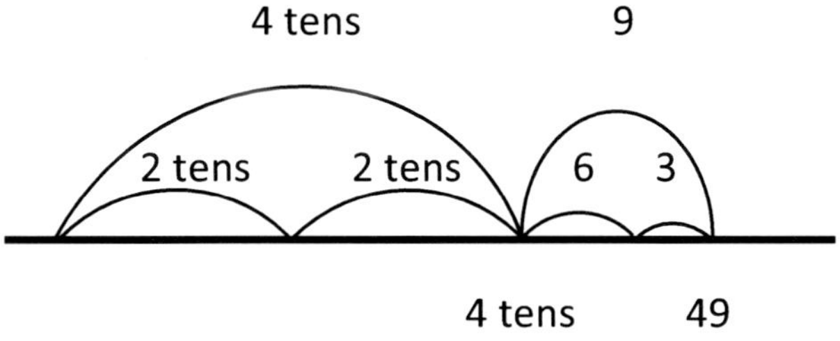

Turn and talk to your partner again. How is Rafi's strategy like Riley's and how is it different?

Author's notes

Anna represents splitting on the open number line. While this is a common strategy that children construct, it is not the most efficient as it results in several numbers to keep in mind.

C15: Strategies for Addition to 100 (Splitting, Associative & Commutative Properties)

This string is like C14, but a discussion of the commutative and associative properties will likely emerge as well.

The String

10 + 10
8 + 1
18 + 11
28 + 31
21 + 38
1 + 8
22 + 28
64 + 37

C16: Strategies for Addition to 100 (Splitting, Associative & Commutative Properties)

This string is like C14.

The String

30 + 20
7 + 2
32 + 27
37 + 22
51 + 19
59 + 11
9 + 5
55 + 29

C17: Strategies for Addition to 100 (Splitting, Associative & Commutative Properties)

This string is like C14.

The String

20 + 30
2 + 5
25 + 32
3 + 7
43 + 37
47 + 33
45 + 34
57 + 24

C18: Strategies for Addition to 100 (Splitting)

This string is like C14.

The String

1 + 9
51 + 29
59 + 21
40 + 30
45 + 35
5 + 7
45 + 37
67 + 25

C19: Strategies for Addition to 100 (Adding jumps of 10s and adjusting)

This set of strings encourages students to keep one number whole and take leaps of ten and adjust. This challenges students to use an equivalent expression – to jump over and then adjust. For example, to add 19, students could add 20 and then subtract 1. So, 25 + 29 becomes 25 + 30 – 1.

In this first string, the first six problems constitute three pairs – the first of each is used to scaffold for the next. The last two problems invite students to use the strategies of taking leaps of ten and adjusting. No helper problems are provided so students will need to make their own, (38 + 40 + 3) and (47 + 20 – 1).

The String

25 + 10
25 + 9
25 + 30
25 + 29
38 + 40
38 + 39
38 + 43
47 + 19

Inside One Classroom: A Portion of the C19 Minilesson

Anna (the teacher): Here we go with another problem. *(Anna writes 25 + 30 on the board.)* Show me with your thumbs when you are ready.

Theo: That's 55. I started with 25 and then added 3 tens, so 35, 45, 55. *(Anna records Theo's strategy on the open number line.)*

Riya: I got 55 too, but I just jumped 30. I knew that 25 and 30 would be 55. *(Anna shows on the same number line how you could also make a jump of 30 to get to 55.)*

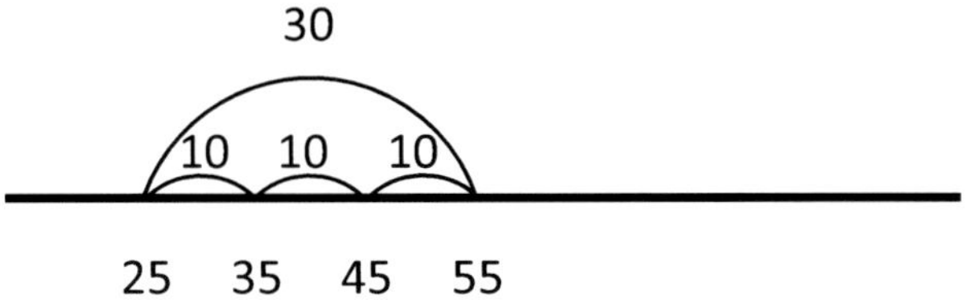

Anna: Here's another one. Everyone ready? *(Anna writes 25 + 29 on the board.)*

Ollie: I'm not sure… that is really tricky!

Anna: It is tricky. Everyone turn and talk to your neighbor about what is happening. How could we solve this problem? Is there anything that could help us? *(Students turn and talk with their partners. After a few minutes, Anna calls them back together.)* Did anyone's partner have a good strategy that you want to share with the group?

Ollie: My partner Jennie said it reminded her of the last problem we did, 25 + 30, because 29 is just one less than 30.

Anna: That's interesting. Tell us more.

Ollie: So… it would just be one less than 25 + 30.

Jennie: Yes! It would be 54. 25 + 30 is 55. Then take away 1… 54!

Anna: Wow. I'm going to record that on the number line. That is super cool! You are telling us to start at 25, jump 30 and then go back 1?

Ollie and Jennie: Uh huh. *(Anna records the representation on the open number line and then resumes pair talk again.)* Turn and talk to your partner again. Help each other understand what Ollie and Jennie are saying.

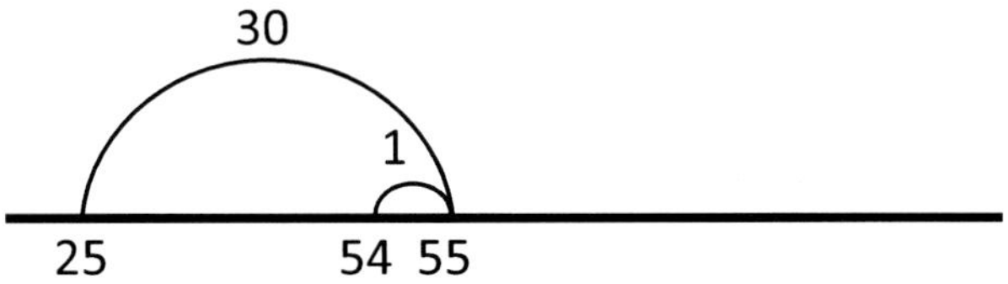

Author's notes

Anna represents Theo's strategy of jumping three tens but then makes sure to show how Riya's strategy of jumping the whole 30 is equivalent (and more efficient) by recording both on the same number line.

Note that Anna allows time for students to talk with their peers about possible strategies and then asks students to share their partner's thinking. This move supports accountable talk.

C20: Strategies for Addition to 100 (Adding jumps of 10s and adjusting)

This string is like C19.

The String

32 + 10

32 + 9

32 + 30

32 + 29

47 + 30

47 + 29

47 + 34

58 + 29

C21: Strategies for Addition to 100 (Adding jumps of 10s and adjusting)

This string is like C19.

The String

54 + 30

54 + 29

54 + 40

54 + 39

54 + 19

72 + 20

72 + 19

63 + 19

C22: Strategies for Addition to 100 (Adding jumps of 10s and adjusting)

This string is like C19.

The String

65 + 10

65 + 9

65 + 20

65 + 19

76 + 20

76 + 19

76 + 25

55 + 39

C23: Strategies for Addition to 100 (Compensation and Associativity)

This next set of strings is focused on compensation and associativity. The strategy focuses on keeping one number whole and decomposing the other addend to get to a landmark number.

In this string, the first problem (29 + 1) is used for support. The second problem is just 10 more. The third problem encourages students to make use of the landmark number 50 by taking 2 from the other addend. The fourth and fifth problems build upon this understanding of getting to a landmark number, but the addend with a 4 in the ones place must be decomposed further. The last problem does not have a helper problem and asks students to make their own.

The String

29 + 1

29 + 11

48 + 12

48 + 22

48 + 4

48 + 34

29 + 22

C24: Strategies for Addition to 100 (Compensation and Associativity)

This string is like C23.

The String

48 + 2

48 + 12

57 + 13

57 + 23

57 + 24

49 + 25

29 + 35

C25: Strategies for Addition to 100 (Compensation and Associativity)

This string is like C23.

The String

46 + 4

46 + 24

57 + 13

57 + 33

57 + 25

68 + 24

46 + 25

C26: Strategies for Addition to 100 (Compensation and Associativity)

This string is like C23.

The String

67 + 3

67 + 13

38 + 12

38 + 22

76 + 8

76 + 18

59 + 34

C27: Strategies for Subtraction within 100 (Jumps of 10 backwards and adjusting)

This string of related problems is designed to encourage students to keep one number whole, take leaps of ten backwards and adjust as needed at the end – to use an equivalent form to simplify the problem. For example, to subtract 29, one might subtract 30 and then add 1.

[Note: If removing or adding on tens is challenging to some students and they count by ones as they remove rather than simply removing 1 from the digit in the tens place, they likely need more work on place value. See the *Around the Circle* minilessons, pages 11-17 in the unit *Minilessons for Extending Addition and Subtraction.* These can be helpful to establish place value patterns and ease with subtracting ten and multiples of tens. You'll find it helpful to do these first and then return to this section.]

As this string is designed to encourage students to keep the one number whole and take leaps of ten back, the first problem sets this up. The second problem is 1 less than the first, and is paired with the first to include adjusting by adding 1 back in. The third and fourth are paired in a similar way. The fifth and sixth require students to make their own helper problems (68 – 30 and 83 – 40).

The String

22 – 10

22 – 9

48 – 20

48 – 19

68 – 29

83 – 39

Inside One Classroom: A Portion of the C27 Minilesson

Anna (the teacher): Everybody ready? Here's the first one: 22 - 10. Show me with a thumbs-up when you are ready. *(Thumbs go up quickly.)*

Eli: It's 12! I knew that. It was easy.

Anna: Those tens can make problems easier! *(Anna draws the jump of 10 backwards on the number line.)*

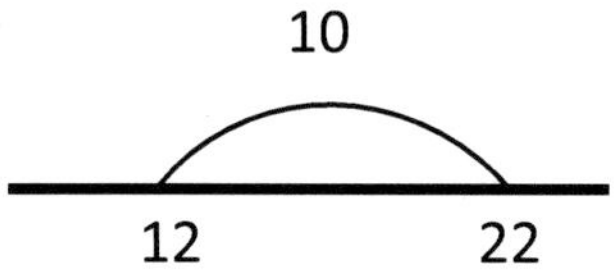

Anna: Let's keep our tens in mind when we do the next problem. Here we go: 22 – 9. Show me with a thumbs-up when you are ready.

Frannie: I know that 9 is one less than 10. The last problem was 12 – 10.

Anna: I like how you are thinking about that 10. I want to record your thinking. Are you saying we should use the last problem to help us?

Frannie: Yes.

Annie. Okay, we have 22 and we are going to jump back 10 to 12. Now what should I do?

Frannie: Make another jump of one.

Anna: Which direction?

Frannie: Backwards.

Annie: *(Records her thinking. Jumping another 1 backwards as Frannie said, so 11 are being taken away.)* Like this?

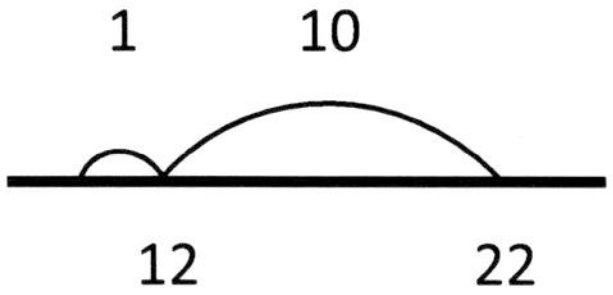

Frannie: I don't think that's right. That's 11.

Helena: It should go the other way. You need to jump up 1 to make it a 9.

Author's notes

Notice that Anna records Frannie's thinking on the open number line even when it is wrong. Instead of just telling Frannie that it is wrong, she uses this opportunity to engender puzzlement and reflection thereby heightening an exploration on the strategy of adjusting. She records Helena's idea but then also returns to Frannie to see if she agrees. In doing so, Anna fosters a mathematical community that sees mistakes as an opportunity to further everyone's understanding.

Anna: Oh, so like this? *(Anna draws the one jump going up the number line.)* 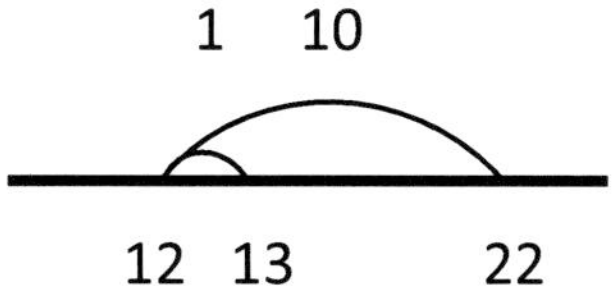 *(Helena nods her head. Lots of the kids nod their heads. Anna turns to Frannie.)* Frannie, what do you think? **Frannie:** Yes, I see! It's 13 and that's one more than 12 because we only took away 9.	

C28: Strategies for Subtraction from 100 (Jumps of 10 backwards and adjusting)

This string is like C27.

The String

36 – 10
36 – 9
43 – 20
43 – 19
65 – 30
65 – 29

C29: Strategies for Subtraction from 100 (Jumps of 10 backwards and adjusting)

This string is like C27.

The String

51 – 10
51 – 9
51 – 20
51 – 19
71 – 29
94 – 49

C30: Strategies for Subtraction from 100 (Jumps of 10 backwards and adjusting)

This string is like C27.

The String

37 – 10

37 – 9

37 – 20

37 – 19

37 – 21

54 – 40

54 – 39

C31: Strategies for Subtraction from 100 (Constant Difference, Equivalence)

This set of strings encourages students to explore constant difference – making problems friendlier by using an equivalent expression, such as using 26 –10 to solve 25 – 9. As you go through the string, record students' strategies on an open number line. You will likely find that strategies will be quite diverse. For example, 15 – 10 may be thought of as removal of 2 fives or removal of one 10. Others may think of it as a missing addend problem: 10 + ? = 15, or as the difference or distance between 10 and 15. Record what children say and do so on the open number line. As you work through the string, students will start to notice interesting relationships, for example that 14 - 9 = 15 - 10. Support conversation on why this is and provide sufficient pair talk and discussion on this continuing to represent both removal and difference models to align with what students offer. At some point in the discussion however, it is important to represent the problems on the number line as difference, *not as removal.* It is usually easier for students to see the equivalence of the expressions as just a slide on the number line to a place that makes the difference easier to solve. With this model they come to see that the difference stays constant, and one can slide the problem to the right or to the left without the difference changing. The figures below show how subtraction as difference and subtraction as removal are recorded differently for 25 – 9.

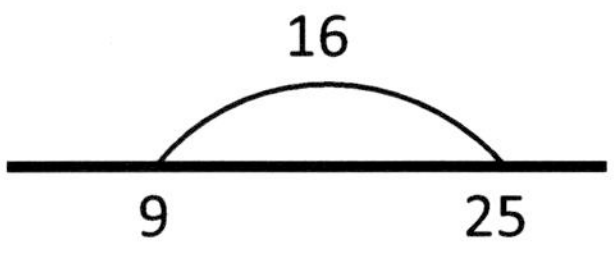

Subtraction as Difference

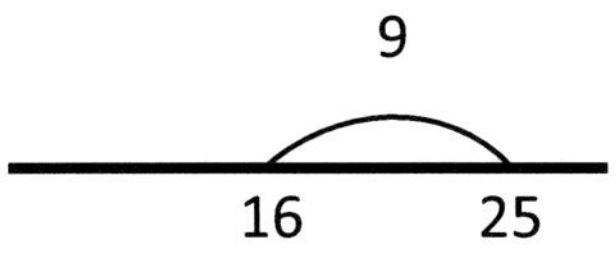

Subtraction as Removal

It can also be helpful to think about constant difference in relation to age. "Sophia is 15 years old; her brother is ten. They are 5 years apart. Next year, she will be 16 and he will be 11. Since they both grow one year, they will still be 5 years apart." The open number line can be described as a timeline.

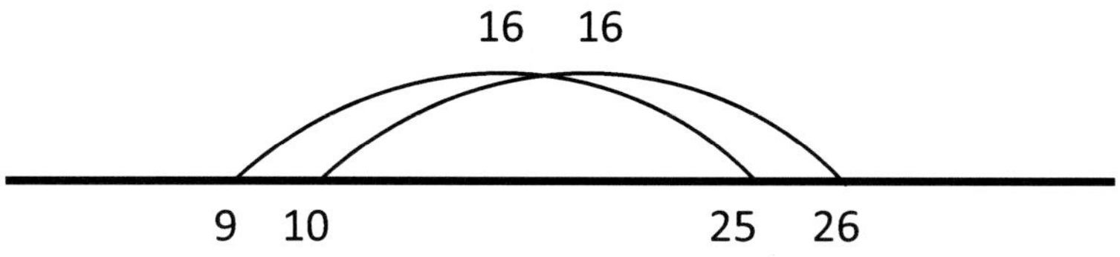

The first problems in string C80 are all related in ways that will support and encourage students to think about constant difference. As students share their strategies, represent their thinking on the open number line. Before you get to the last problem promote discussion on why some of the answers are the same. Wonder why and promote inquiry on this question. Provide pair talk, exploring these equivalent expressions as just sliding up and down while the difference between the numbers is staying the same. Then challenge students to find an easy equivalent expression to solve 41 – 29. Some students will likely suggest 40 – 28, while others will offer 42 – 30. Explore which is easier. While they are both equivalent and can be used, it is often easier to solve problems where the subtrahend (in contrast to the minuend) is a landmark. You may also find that students overgeneralize the use of compensation and offer 40 - 30, which worked for addition but won't work for subtraction because the difference is no longer constant. There are big ideas about subtraction here so allow students to become puzzled and support inquiry and reflection. Foster enjoyment throughout the inquiry and let them invent and justify their conclusions. This is a place for the Standards of Mathematical Practice to really come alive.

The String

15 – 10
14 – 9
26 – 10
25 – 9
44 – 20
43 – 19
42 – 18
41 – 29

C32: Strategies for Subtraction from 100 (Constant Difference, Equivalence)

This string is like C31.

The String

23 – 10

22 – 9

35 – 10

34 – 9

35 – 20

34 – 19

33 – 18

C33: Strategies for Subtraction from 100 (Constant Difference, Equivalence)

This string is like C31.

The String

45 – 30

44 – 29

43 – 28

59 – 30

58 – 29

57 – 28

54 - 39

C34: Constant Difference, Equivalence

This string is like C31.

The String

72 – 50

70 – 48

71 – 49

84 – 60

82 – 58

83 – 59

79 – 36

C35: Mystery Numbers

This set of strings involves solving for mystery numbers. For these problems, provide notepaper and pens, or small whiteboards and markers. Tell students that the question mark (?) is a mystery number that they need to find, and suggest they use the open number line as a tool for thinking. For example, students may jump up 2 to get to 20 and then 5 more to get to 25, or remove 5 from 25 and then 2, making the mystery number 7 to solve 25 - ? = 18, or 18 + ? = 25. Or, they might use constant difference to solve 25 – 18 as 27 – 20. This is a nice chance for them to show you what they know and to assess their ability to use a model as a tool for thinking.

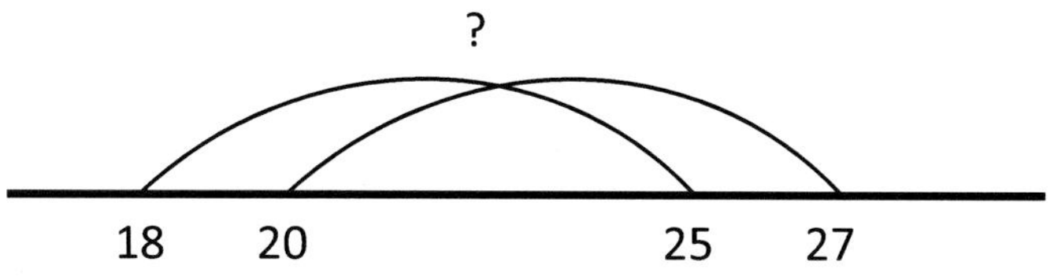

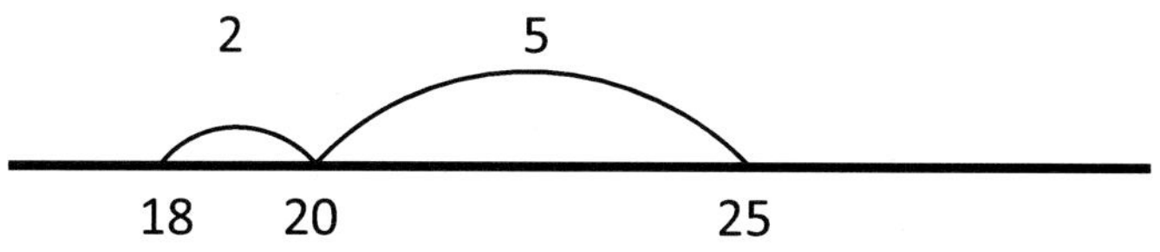

The String

25 - ? = 18

18 + ? = 25

40 - ? = 15

25 + ? = 40

? + 35 = 50

36 + ? = 51

? + 49 = 64

C36: Mystery Numbers

This string is like C35. Notice that it focuses on getting to landmark numbers, and prioritizing 5s and 10s. The first problem 17 + ? = 30, asks students to think how many more to the next ten, 3 and then add 10 more. The second problem asks them to build upon the last but this time extends up to 32. Students will often jump 3 first to the 10, add 10 and then 2 more to get to 32.

The String

17 + ? = 30

? + 17 = 32

17 + ? = 52

? + 26 = 51

26 + ? = 71

37 + ? = 72

C37: Mystery Numbers

This string is like C35.

The String

? + 18 = 25

? + 8 = 25

28 + ? = 45

? + 35 = 50

37 + ? = 52

37 + ? = 72

C38: Mystery Numbers

This string is like C35.

The String

39 + ? = 50

? + 29 = 50

29 + ? = 54

50 + ? = 75

? + 49 = 75

59 + ? = 92

Beyond Arithmetic

Exploring Space and Shapes

D1: Pathways Traveled (Quadrilaterals)

The strings in this first part of section D focus on navigational pathways of straight distances and turns that enclose space and can be used to describe, name, and categorize 2-dimensional shapes. This is an important developmental step as eventually these will come to be understood as line segments and angles.

To begin, each student should have a blank piece of paper and a sharpie with a clipboard, or a small whiteboard and marker. Tell students that they are going to be drawing a shape. You will tell them how many straight lines and how many turns they should make to get back to the starting place. Give students a few minutes to complete their work. If some complete it quickly, ask them to explore if there are other ways to follow the same directions, reminding them that they need to end where they started.

Afterwards, have several students share what polygon they think they made and their thinking. Take a picture and display it from your computer onto your smartboard. Because measurements of the turns and straight sides are not given, there are many types of quadrilaterals in this first set that are possible. Have several shared and displayed and create a discussion on how they are similar, eventually naming all the responses that have 4 sides and 4 turns with the starting and endpoint at the same place as quadrilaterals.

The String

Draw 4 straights and 4 turns to get back to your starting place.
What shape did you make? How do you know?

D2: Pathways Traveled (Triangles)

This string is like D1 except that it focuses on triangles.

The String

Draw 3 straights and 3 turns to get back to your starting place.
What shape did you make? How do you know?

D3: Pathways Traveled (Squares)

This string is like D1 except that the lengths and the turns all need to be equal. Here the directions will all create squares, but they can be different sizes. This is an opportunity to talk about how squares all have 4 equal sides and 4 equal turns. The lengths determine the size of the square (small to large), but the shapes are all squares. [Note: They are also quadrilaterals and rectangles.]

The String

Draw 4 straights all the same length and 4 turns all the same size to get back to your starting place.
What shape have you made? How do you know?

Inside One Classroom: A Portion of the D1 Minilesson

Anna: *(Anna writes the directions on the board. Reads them and gives the students some time to work on their drawings.)* Show me with a thumb when you are ready to share.

Alex: I made a square.

Anna: *(Anna projects Alex's drawing.)* Tell us more.

Alex: I know that squares have four sides and four corners. So, I started here. *(Alex points to his starting point.)* And I drew four straights and four turns just like a square.

Anna: *(Turns to the class.)* What does everyone think?

Fiona: All the sides are the same! So, it is a square. But you don't need to make them all the same. I made some of my sides long.

Anna: (*Anna projects Fiona's drawing.)* What do you notice about Fiona's drawing?

Esteban: There are four sides too, but 2 of them are very long. It's a rectangle.

Anna: That's interesting. So, do both rectangles and squares have four straight sides and four corners? (*Most of the class nods to show agreement.)* So, they are both rectangles, but the square is a special rectangle because the sides are all the same length.

Esteban: Mine looks even more different! *(Anna projects Esteban's drawing.)*

Anna: Turn and talk with your partner. What do you think? *(Anna gives the students time to talk and goes around to listen to what they are saying.)* Let's share. What did you notice?

Kaia: It kind of looks like a diamond!

Fiona: The turns are different!

Anna: That's interesting. *(Anna puts both Esteban, Fiona, and Alex's drawings side by side.)* What do you notice about the turns?

Fiona: With the rectangles, the turns were the same. With Esteban's, some turns were big, and others were small.

Anna: Mathematicians call all these shapes quadrilaterals. That word just means 4 sides and 4 turns back to the starting place. The sides don't have to be the same length, but they could be. And the turns don't have to be the same, but they could be. Quadrilaterals just have 4 straights and 4 turns.

Author's notes

Anna uses the students' work to focus on a big idea. All the directions say are 4 straight paths and 4 turns. The shape is a quadrilateral, but could be a square, rectangle, rhombus or trapezoid, etc. By examining the students' work, Anna helps keep the focus on the similarities and differences and the attributes.

D4: Pathways Traveled (Rectangles)

This string is like D1. Here the directions will all create rectangles including squares, and different sizes are possible. This is an opportunity to talk about how squares are rectangles but not all rectangles are squares. All have 4 straights and 4 equal turns. These are complex understandings for first grade that the students can begin to think about, although they are not required to fully understand the logic until later grades.

The String

Draw 4 straights and 4 turns all the same size. The straights don't have to all be the same length, but the turns do all need to be the same and you still must get back to your starting place.
What shape have you made? How do you know?

D5: Pathways Traveled (Pentagons)

This string is like D1, but it focuses on pentagons.

The String

Draw 5 straights and 5 turns to get back to your starting place.
What shape have you made? How do you know?

D6: Pathways Traveled (Hexagons)

This string is like D1, but it focuses on hexagons.

The String

Draw 6 straights and 6 turns to get back to your starting place.
What shape have you made? How do you know?

D7: Quick Images with Shapes

Each of the strings in this next section is crafted as a series of quick images. **You can find PowerPoints to display the shapes on P2S2 (the New Perspectives Online platform) under Online Resources in the unit *Shaping Up the Yard*.** Ask students to consider the name of the shape and more importantly to describe the shape they saw and justify how they knew it was that shape. Invite a few students to share their answers and provide pair talk. Focus the discussion on the attributes of the shapes – the sides and corners.

Images #1 and #2 are the same triangle, but it has been rotated 180 degrees. Image #3 is also a triangle, but a right triangle. The goal here is to have students see that the 3 corners and 3 sides make it a triangle, not the orientation or length of the sides. Images #4 and #5 also allow students to explore orientation but with a square. See Appendix A for a larger version of these images.

The String

Image #1

Image #2

Image #3

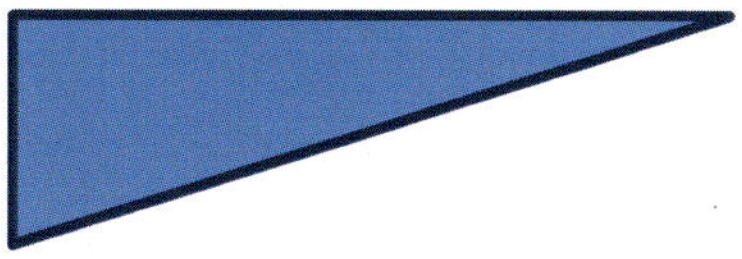

Image #4

Image #5

D8: Quick Images with Shapes

This string focuses on 4-sided shapes, quadrilaterals. Image #1 begins with a square. Image #2 plays with its orientation. Image #3 is a rhombus which also builds upon image #2 which is a square but also a rhombus. A square can be a rhombus. But a rhombus is not always a square! The other images extend the four-sided shapes to consider parallelograms and trapezoids. See Appendix B for a larger version of these images.

The String

Image #1

Image #2

Image #3

Image #4

Image #5

Inside One Classroom: A Portion of the D8 Minilesson

Anna (the teacher): *(Shows image #2 briefly.)* What shape do you think this is? How do you know? Show me with a thumb when you are ready to share.

Riya: That's a diamond!

Anna: Tell us more about that.

Riya: It's pointy at the top and pointy at the bottom, just like a diamond.

Anna: *(To the class.)* What do you think?

Nikki: I think it's a square! It has four equal sides just like the last one. It is just turned to the side.

Anna*: (Anna shows image #2 again and rotates it back so it looks like image #1. She turns to the class.)* Do you agree? *(Most of the class nods.)* Turn and talk to a partner about that. *(Anna moves around and listens in on conversations until everyone agrees.)* Okay. Here's another one. *(Anna shows image #3 briefly.)* Show me with a thumb when you are ready to share... Fabian, start us off.

Fabian: It has four sides. But I don't think it's a square anymore. Can you turn it on its side? *(Anna turns Image #3 so one straight side is aligned with the bottom of the board.)*

Fabian: Nope. It's not a square.

Anna: Hmmm. Why not? Are the sides all equal?

Fabian: That's funny. I think so!!

Anna: Let's turn and talk about this with a partner. What makes this different from a square? *(Anna gives the students sufficient time to talk, moving around and listening to their conversations.)* Okay – let's come back together. What do you think?

Kia: A square has all the sides the same. This one does too. But the corners are different.

Raffi: I think it's a rhombus. It's just like the white one in our pattern blocks.

Anna: This is so interesting! We have two shapes where the sides are the same, but the corners are different. We know one is a square and think the other may be a rhombus. These are important things we are noticing. I wonder... do you think the square might also be a rhombus? Hmmm... is it also a quadrilateral? Turn and talk about that.

Author's notes

Anna rotates the images to compare the shapes, reinforcing that orientation will not change the shape but may make it easier to analyze.

A square can be a rhombus, but a rhombus is not always a square! This is developmentally a complex big idea for 1st graders—one that they are not expected to understand fully now but can begin to explore.

D9: Quick Images with Shapes

This string focuses on hexagons. Here the focus is again on the attributes – the sides and corners. Hexagons can look different but if they have 6 sides and 6 corners, and the shape is closed, they are still hexagons. The last two images offer an examination of the properties. Image #4 asks students to focus on sides and corners and it is likely not a recognizable shape for most first graders. Focus discussion on the number of sides and the number of corners. Image #5 introduces the pentagon for comparison. See Appendix C for a larger version of these images.

The String

Image #1

Image #2

Image #3

Image #4

Image #5

D10: Quick Images with Shapes

This string is like D9, but the first three images focus on the properties of triangles. The last two provide 4-sided shapes (quadrilaterals) for comparison. See Appendix D for a larger version of these images.

The String

Image #1

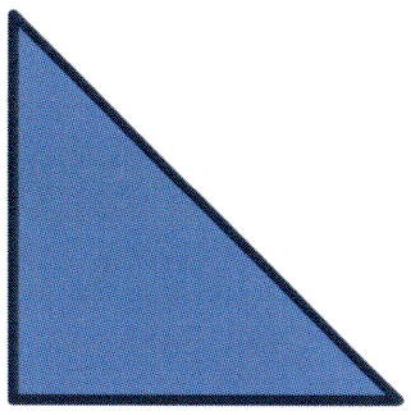

Image #2

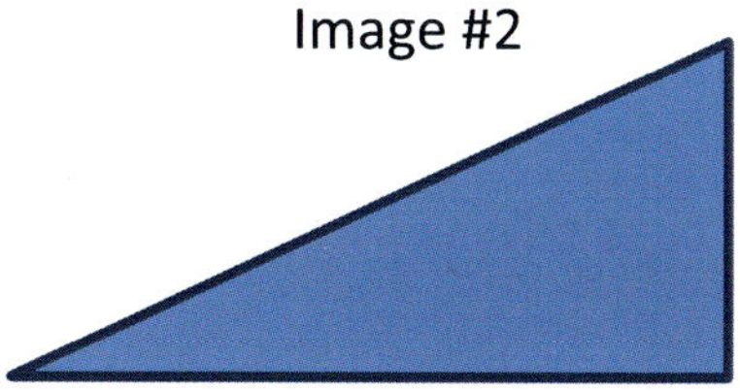

Image #3

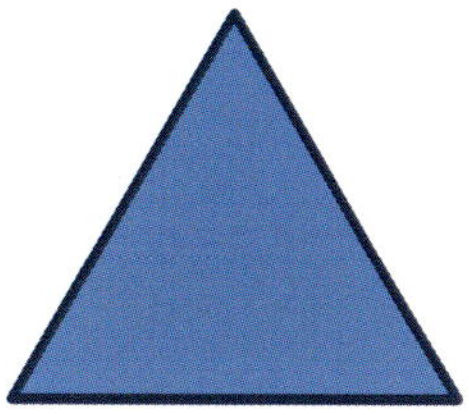

Image #4

Image #5

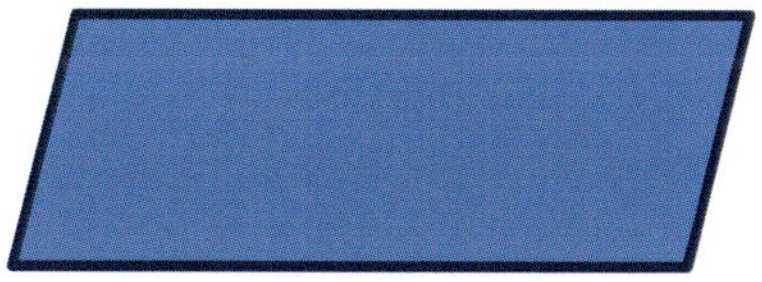

D11: Quick Images with Shapes

The first three images focus on pentagons. The first is a regular pentagon. The other two are irregular pentagons, asking students to focus on the common attributes – 5 sides and 5 corners. Image #4 provides a regular hexagon for comparison and image #5 asks students to contemplate a quite irregular hexagon. See Appendix E for a larger version of these images.

The String

Image #1

Image #2

Image #3

Image #4

Image #5

D12: Composing/Decomposing Shapes

For this set of strings, students work with quick images of pattern blocks to compose and decompose shapes. Provide each student with a small set of pattern blocks. See Appendix F for a larger version of these images.

For this string, show each image briefly. Ask students what shape they see if they were to draw around the whole shape. Then ask them what other shapes could be used to make it. For some shapes such as the hexagon, there will be several different composition possibilities. Make sure to have several students share their ideas. For each one, model the thinking by laying other pattern blocks over the initial shape. For example, all three shapes can be made using only green triangles, but the hexagon can also be made with two red trapezoids, or with two blue rhombi and 2 green triangles.

The String

Image #1

Image #2

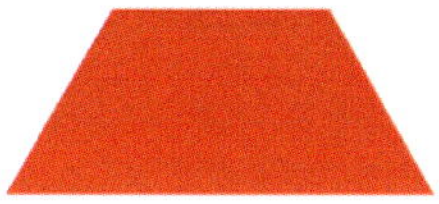

Image #3

Image #4

D13: Composing/Decomposing Shapes

This string focuses on composing and decomposing of the regular hexagon. Briefly show image #1 and have students identify that it is a hexagon and explain why. For the next images show the hexagon along with the other shape to its right and ask students how many are needed to create a hexagon. For each one, model the thinking on the projector by laying the other pattern blocks over the initial shape. See Appendix G for a larger version of these images.

The String

Image #1

Image #2

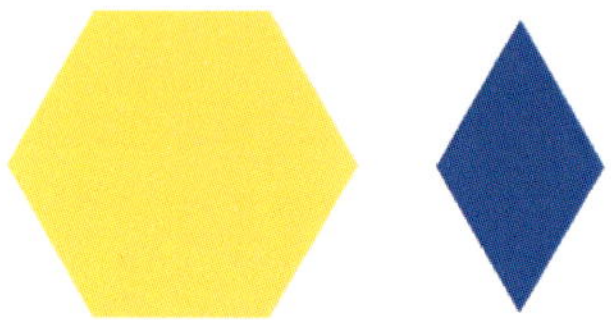

Image #3

Image #4

Image #5

D14: Composing/Decomposing Shapes

For this string, project the pattern block pattern briefly on the projector using Appendix H. Ask students to describe what shapes they saw and what big shape is made if they were to trace around the outside.

The String

Image #1

Image #2

Image #3

Image #4

D15: Quick Images with Faces of Solids

Materials Needed

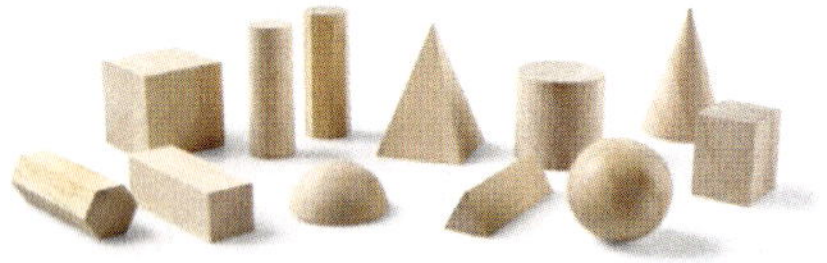

Strings D15-D19 require a set of 3-D solids for students to see.

These strings focus on the properties of solids. They support students in analyzing the solids by focusing on the faces. For these strings, lay out a set of 3-D solids that the students can see. The set should include a cube, cone, rectangular prism, triangular prism, cylinder, sphere, and square pyramid. Then show a quick image of the face in the string for a few seconds and then remove it. Ask students to think about which of the 3-D solids from the set would have a matching face. Have them turn and talk to their neighbor about which solid could have made that footprint and how. Invite a few children to share their answers and check out their predictions by placing the solid on the shape. Make sure that when there is more than one possibility, students have a chance to see both and compare.

This string begins with a square. It could be the bottom, top, or side of the cube; the bottom of the square pyramid; or the side of the triangular prism, etc. The second image is the triangle, it could be a face on the square pyramid, the bottom of the triangular prism, etc. As you work through the minilesson, it is important to discuss a variety of possible choices and focus discussion on the properties and attributes of the shapes and solids. See Appendix I for a larger version of these images.

The String

Image #1

Image #2

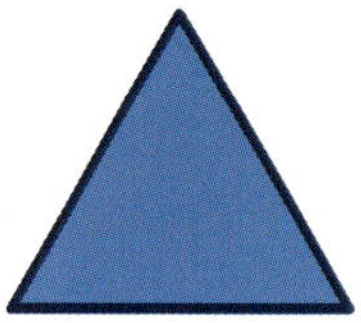

Image #3

Image #4

Inside One Classroom: A Portion of the D15 Minilesson

Anna (the teacher): *(Briefly shows Image #1.)* What shape did you see? How do you know? Show me with your thumbs when you have an idea...Emma?

Emma: It's a square. That's an easy one. It has four sides!

Anna: Wiggle your pinkies if you agree with Emma. *(Most of the class wiggles their pinkies.)* Okay, now what solid do you think might have a square as a face? Show me with your thumbs when you are ready. *(Waits until most thumbs are up.)* Turn and talk with your neighbor. What do you think? Why? *(After some time for discussion, Anna calls them back together.)* Who can explain what your partner was thinking?

Isaac: Elsie said it's the cube: there's a square on each side.

Anna: Interesting. Let's check. *(Anna holds up the cube and places one side on the quick image of the square.)* Elsie – what do you think?

Elsie: It matches. I think there are four squares. See all the sides.

Rayna: But you are missing the top and the bottom. There are six. The sides are four and then there are two more – the top and bottom. 6!

Anna: Wiggle your pinkies if you think there are 6. *(Most wiggle their pinkies.)* Let's check. *(Anna moves the cube touching each face to the square and the class counts together.)* 1, 2, 3, 4, 5, 6. So the cube has 6 faces that are squares. Does any other shape have a face that is square?

Eduardo: Yes! The rectangle one.

Anna: *(Anna holds up the rectangular prism.)* This one? The rectangular prism?

Raffi: I don't think so. That has rectangles.

Anna: Eduardo, what do you think?

Eduardo: If you turn it on its side, it has a square and there's another one too.

Anna: *(Anna lays the rectangular prism down showing it matches on two sides.)* Fascinating. There are two different solids that have squares for their faces – the cube and the rectangular prism! How is the cube related to the rectangular prism? Turn and talk with your neighbor.

Author's notes

The string focuses students on the properties of the shapes and solids shown. The quick images ask students to consider the attributes of the faces on the solids.

Anna acknowledges both solids - the cube and rectangular prism and then challenges the class to consider others that might have square faces.

D16: Quick Images with Faces of Solids

This string is like D15. See Appendix J for a larger version of these images.

The String

Image #1

Image #2

Image #3

Image #4

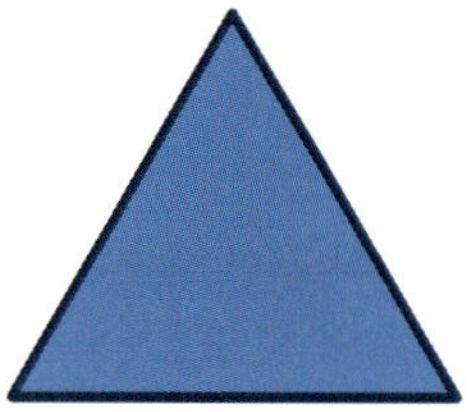

D17: Quick Images with Nets of Solids

Display a set of 3-D solids that the students can see. The set should include a cube, cone, rectangular prism, triangular prism, cylinder, sphere, and square pyramid. Tell students you are going to show them a net of a solid. Explain that a net shows all the faces of a 3-dimensional shape laid flat in 2-dimensional form. Show the net image briefly. Ask students what shapes they saw. Then ask them what solid they think has all these faces. Have students turn and talk with each other and then share and justify their ideas. Have a copy of the net available so that you can fold it at the end to show students how it becomes a solid. See Appendix K for a larger version of the net.

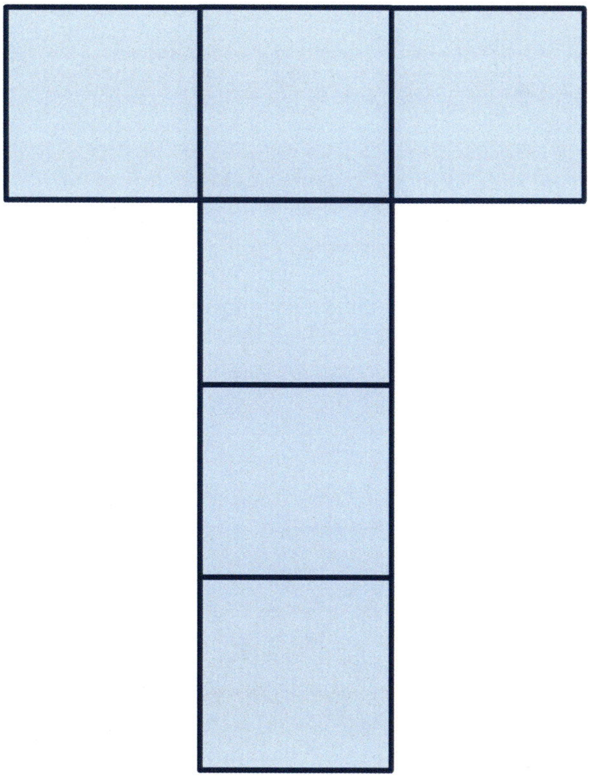

D18: Quick Images with Nets of Solids

This string is like D17. A cube is not produced, however; the non-cube rectangular prism is produced. See Appendix L for a larger version of the net.

D19: Quick Images with Nets of Solids

This string is like D17. See Appendix M for a larger version of the net.

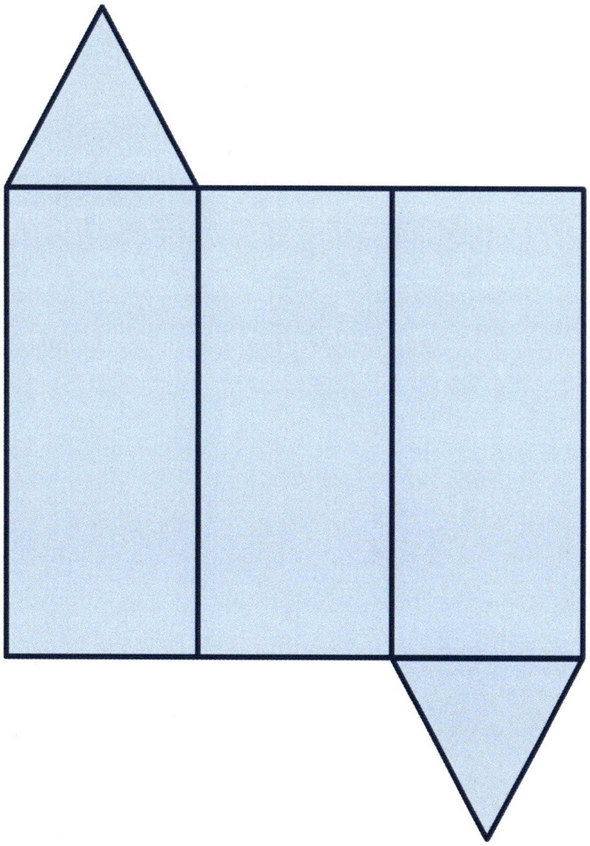

D20: Partitioning Shapes (circles, halves and fourths)

This string focuses on partitioning a circle. Tell the students you are going to be dividing a circle into equal shares. Show each image briefly. Ask students if the shares are portioned equally; are they fair?

In this string, the first two images deal with halves. The first is not portioned equally, the second is. For the second, if the students do not bring up the terminology halves, this is an opportunity to talk about this. The last three images work with fourths or quarters. The third image is not equal, but both the fourth and fifth are, even though the fifth image has a different orientation. Again, make sure to introduce 'fourths' and 'quarters' into the discussion if the students do not bring it up themselves. See Appendix N for a larger version of these images.

The String

Image #1

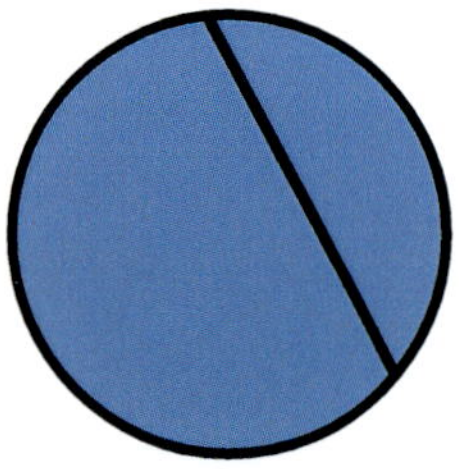

Image #2

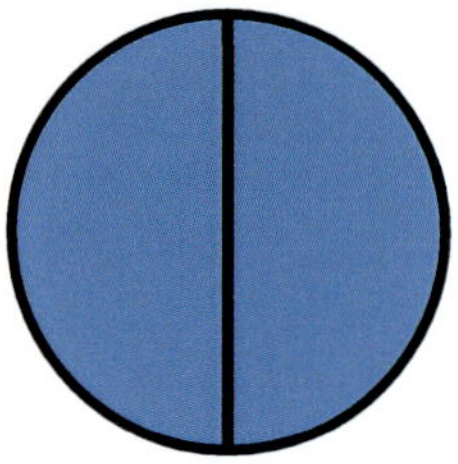

Image #3

Image #4

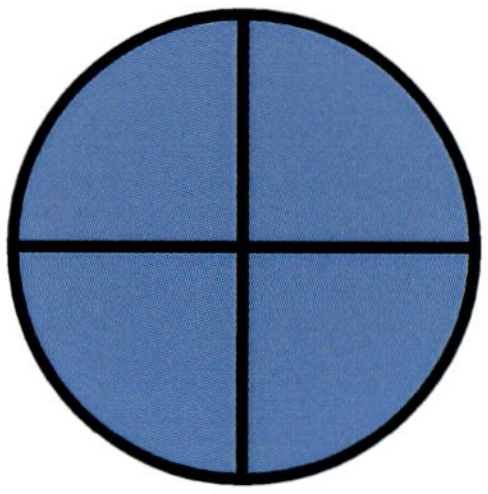

Image #5

D21: Partitioning Shapes (rectangles, halves)

Tell students you are going to be partitioning a rectangle into equal shares. Show each image briefly. Ask students if the shares are portioned equally; are they fair? Ask them to justify their answers.

In this string, the images focus on dividing the rectangle into two equal parts, halves. The first is not partitioned equally horizontally, but the second is. The third image is not partitioned equally vertically, but the fourth is. The fifth image asks students to consider a different type of partition, but one that is still equal. See Appendix O for a larger version of these images.

The String

Image #1

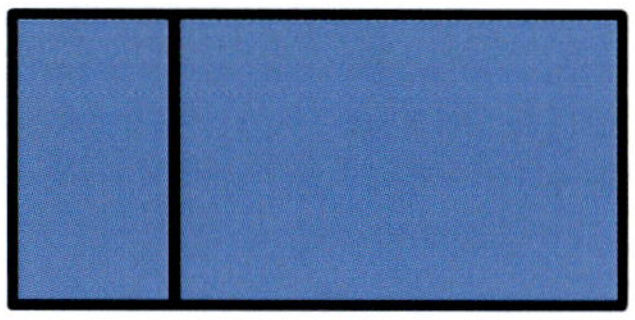

Image #2

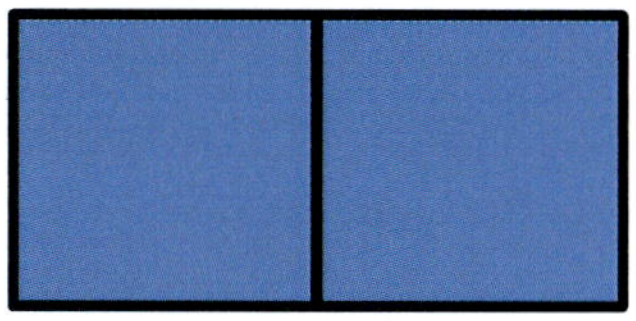

Image #3

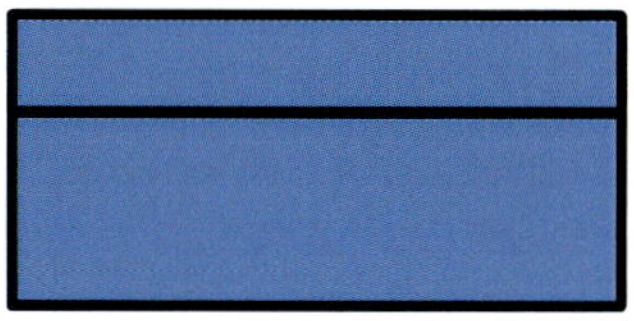

Image #4

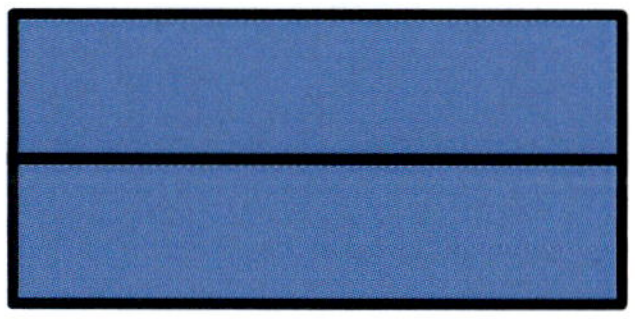

Image #5

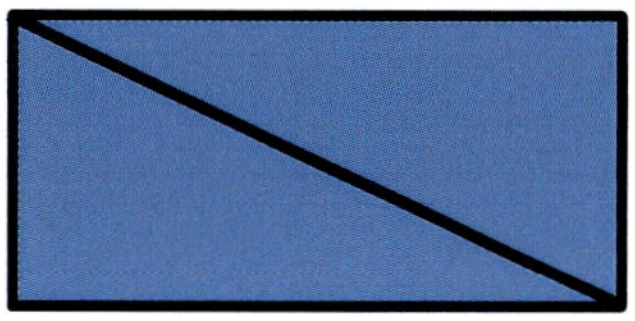

D22: Partitioning Shapes (rectangles, fourths)

Tell students you are going to be partitioning a rectangle into equal shares. Show each image briefly. Ask students if the shares are portioned equally, are they fair? Ask them to justify their answers.

In this string, the images focus on dividing the rectangle into four equal parts, fourths or quarters. The first is not partitioned equally horizontally, but the second is. The third image is not partitioned equally vertically, but the fourth is. See Appendix P for a larger version of these images.

The String

Image #1

Image #2

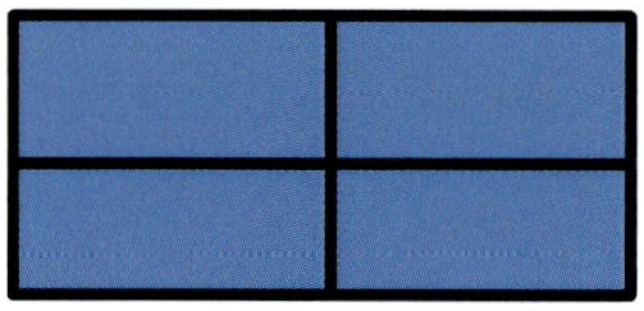

Image #3

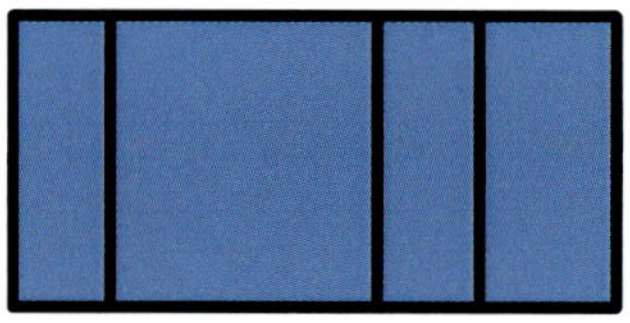

Image #4

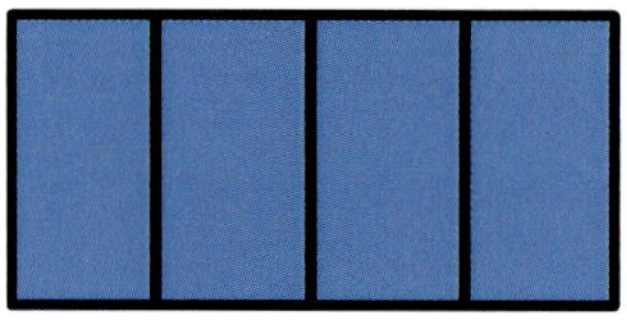

D23: Partitioning Shapes (circles, halves, fourths)

This string works with circles, halves, and fourths. Show each image briefly. For the first image, ask students what shape they see. For the next three images ask students how much of the blue circle is left and how they know. Have students share their thinking. This is an opportunity to talk about halves, fourths and quarters. For image #3, there is one quarter or one fourth left out of four fourths. For image #4, there are three quarters, or three fourths, left out of four fourths. See Appendix Q for a larger version of these images.

The String

Image #1

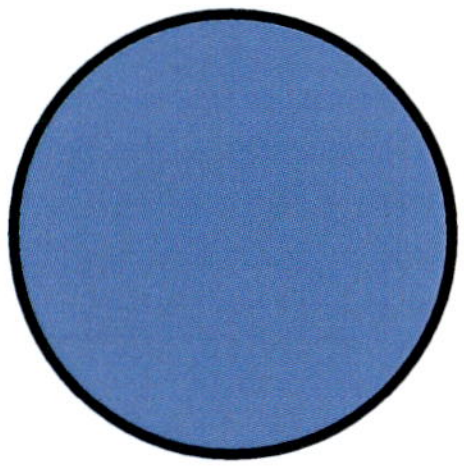

Image #2

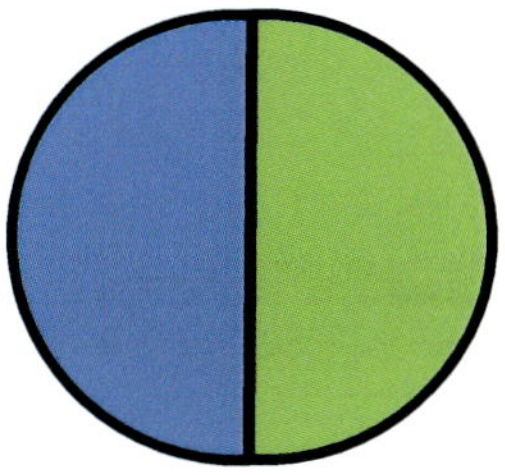

Image #3

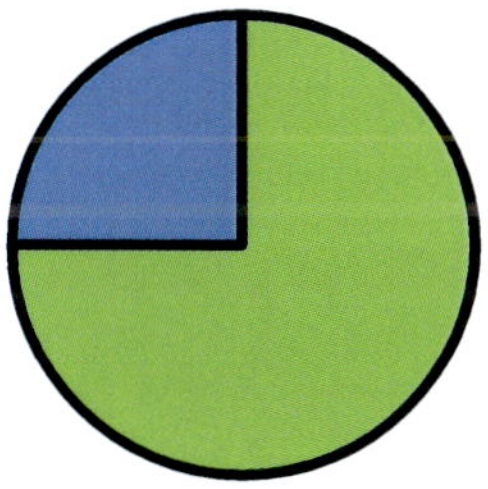

Image #4

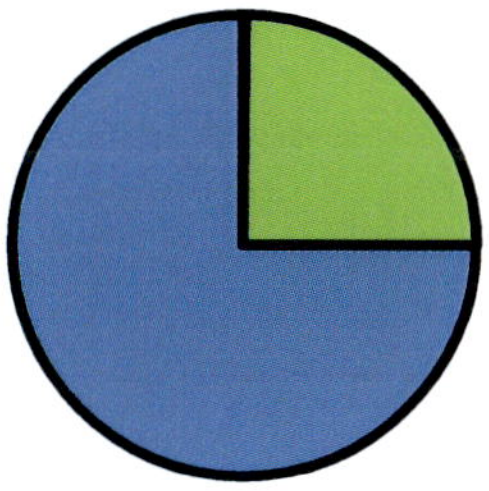

E1: Comparing Lengths

These strings use Cuisenaire rods to compare lengths. As quick images, show each of the rod comparisons below. Leave the rods used visible as you go, asking each time: Which is longer? How do you know? Add the appropriate magnitude sign (<, >) during the discussion. The purpose of these minilessons is to support the logic of transitivity. If brown is < than blue, and black is < than brown, then black is < than blue. Don't show the picture below, only show the rods in the string. The picture is shown below for you only. Encourage children to use reasoning to defend their thinking.

The String

Black and Orange rods

Black and Brown and Orange rods

Brown and Blue rods

Show only Blue but ask about Black and Blue

Show only Black, but ask about Black and Blue

Show only Blue, but ask about Orange and Blue

After the discussion on all the above comparisons ask the following questions (without showing the picture of all the rods):

Can you tell which color rod is the longest without me showing you?
Which is the shortest? How do you know?
If we ordered the rods in the string shortest to tallest, which would be first?
Which would be second?
Could we put the rods together like a staircase? What order would they go in?

Inside One Classroom: A Portion of the E1 Minilesson

Anna (the teacher): Here we go with the first one. Is everybody ready? *(Anna briefly shows the black and orange rods.)* Which rod is longer? How do you know?

Margie: I know. The black is short! The orange is long!

Anna: Could we say that the orange is longer than the black? And that the black is shorter than the orange? *(Anna writes orange > black, and black < orange.)* Turn and talk about that... *(Anna moves around and listens to the conversations. After some discussion and consensus Anna goes on.)* Okay, here's the next one. *(Anna leaves the rods in place but adds the brown rod, leaving all of them visible briefly.)* Now we have three rods. Which is the longest?

Zac: Orange is the longest.

Allie: And black is still the shortest!

Anna: What about the brown one?

Zac: That's longer than the black one, but shorter than the orange one.

Allie: If you put it in the middle, it's like a staircase.

Anna: Interesting. *(Anna moves the brown rod to the middle.)* So, the brown is longer than the black, and the orange is longer than the brown. *(Anna records within the string using the magnitude signs.)* Okay, here is another one. *(Anna removes the three rods and places just the brown and blue.)* Look quickly! Which is longer? How do you know?

Allie: The blue is longer than the brown.

Anna: Does everyone agree? *(The class nods their heads.)* Now I have a challenge for you. If I only show you the blue, but not the black, can you tell me which is longer? The blue or the black? Turn and talk to your partner. *(Anna moves around listening to different conversations.)* Let's come back together. What did you think? Do we need to see the black next to the blue to tell us which is longer?

Simon: My partner Zelle and I think the black was shorter than the brown. And the brown was shorter than the blue. So, we think blue is longer than black!

Anna: Wow! Are Simon and Zelle right? They did that without looking. How is it possible to know without even looking? Turn and talk about what Simon and Zelle are thinking.

Author's notes

The first image is a quick one meant to be easy. Anna notes Margie's language as she calls one short and one long. Her language is discrete not comparative. When she responds Anna reframes the answers using comparative language, shorter and longer.

By showing only one length, Anna invites the children to consider transitivity, If $a < b$ and $b < c$, then $a < c$. The development of this logic will need time, much thought, and discussion. It is an important big idea on the measurement landscape for your first graders to construct.

E2: Comparing Lengths

This string is like E1. As quick images, show each of the rod comparisons below. Leave the rods used visible as you go and ask each time: Which is longer? How do you know?

The String

Purple and Black
Purple and Yellow and Black
Yellow and Dark Green
Show only Dark Green, but ask about Purple and Dark Green
Show only Purple, but ask about Purple and Dark Green
Show only Dark Green, but ask about Black and Dark Green

After the discussion on all the above comparisons ask:

Can you tell which color rod is the longest without me showing you?
Which is the shortest? How do you know?
If we ordered the rods shortest to tallest, which would be first?
Which would be second?
Could we put the rods together like a staircase? What order would they go in?

E3: Comparing Lengths

As quick images, show each of the Cuisenaire rod comparisons below. Ask each time: Which is longer? How do you know? This string uses the total length of two rods. Make sure to stack them end-to-end so students can compare the total length.

The String

2 Yellow and 1 Orange
2 Dark Green and 1 Orange
2 Purple and 1 Orange
2 Purple and 2 Yellow
2 Dark Green and 2 Purple
Show 2 Dark Green with 2 Purple and ask about 1 Orange.

Can you tell which color rod is the longest without me showing you?
Which is the shortest? How do you know?
If we ordered the rods shortest to tallest, which would be first?
Which would be second?
Could we put the rods together like a staircase? What order would they go in?

E4: Distance Traveled

As quick images, briefly show each set of rods in the string below lined up as a length of fence sections above a line, asking each time: How far are we? How do you know? As students share, record their solutions on a number line, marking the numbers below the rods. The recording below represents a skip counting strategy. The second shows a recording of a regrouping strategy.

The String

4 yellow rods

2 orange rods

2 orange rods and 4 yellow rods

8 yellow rods

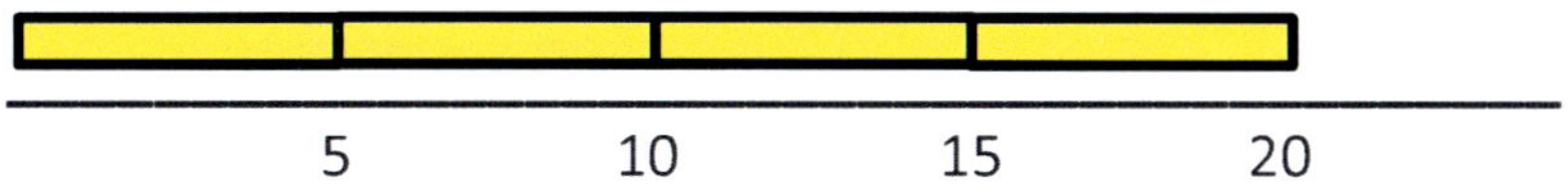

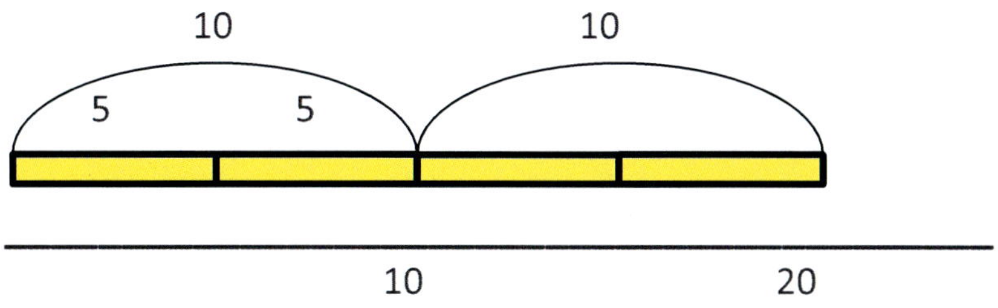

Inside One Classroom: A Portion of the E4 Minilesson

Anna (the teacher): Here's the first one. *(Anna has drawn a long line across the board and shows a quick image of the 4 yellow rods.)* How far have we fenced? How do you know?

Fabian: I know that yellow is 5.

Anna: If each yellow is 5 units long, how far did we fence with the yellow rods?

Berta: The fence is 20. I saw 4 yellow rods. That's 5, 10, 15, 20.

Anna: Wiggle your pinkies if you agree with Berta. *(Most of the class wiggles their pinkies.)* Okay, here's the next one. *(Anna shows a quick image of 2 orange rods above the long line on the board.)* Show me with a thumb when you are ready to share.

Eli: That's the same! It's 20, too.

Anna: Tell me more. Why?

Eli: The orange is 10.

Anna: Interesting. Turn and talk with your partner. Why is a 4-yellow section fence the same length as a 2-orange section fence? *(Anna gives the students time to talk, moving around to listen to different partnerships. She then brings the class back together.)* Alberto, can you share what you discussed with your partner?

Alberto: 2 tens is the same as 4 fives because two 5s make a 10.

Anna: *(Anna shows the image of the 2-orange fence again, this time adding the 4 yellow on top to show how they are equal lengths. She represents Alberto's thinking on the number line below the rods. She also writes the mathematical expression 10 + 10 = (5 + 5) + (5 + 5) on the board.)* So, you are saying that that 2 tens = 4 fives? These are equivalent lengths? Wow!! Ok then, maybe I need a harder one, Here's the next one. *(Anna smiles and displays a fence section 2-orange and 4-yellow long.)* Show me with a thumb when you are ready to share. *(After most thumbs are showing Anna asks them to turn and talk with their partners again. She walks around to listen to different discussions then brings the class together.)* Wow. I've heard lots of interesting discussions about this length. Tomas will you share what you and Berta were discussing?

Tomas: It's so cool. It's double.

Berta: We knew that 2 oranges were 20, and we also knew the 4 yellows were 20, so we doubled and got 40!

Anna: Okay. Let me record your thinking.

Author's notes

Anna uses the number line as a representational model below the rods. She removes the rods between each problem but will bring them back when needed for comparison.

Anna models their thinking by putting the 4 yellow rods on top of the original image - 2 orange rods long. This shows the equivalency that Berta and Tomas are using.

E5: Distance Traveled

The string is like E4. As quick images, briefly show each set of rods in the list below lined up as a length of fence sections above a line. Ask each time: How far are we? How do you know? As students share, record their solutions on a number line, marking the numbers below the rods and the jumps (if and when they regroup) above.

The String

3 orange rods

6 yellow rods

3 orange rods and 4 yellow rods

10 yellow rods

E6: Distance Traveled

This is like E4.

The String

4 yellow rods

4 yellow rods and 1 purple

2 orange rods and 1 purple

6 purple rods

E7: Time (within a minute)

It is best to do this string after the unit *The Timekeepers*, not before. String an alternating length of 60 connecting cubes (5 red, 5 white, 5 red, 5 white, etc.) above a strip of adding machine paper. Mark the strip at the end with a line, and on the bottom write 60 seconds. Explain that this is a timeline. Remind students that time is measured in seconds and minutes and that 60 seconds is one minute long. Mark one minute at the end of the line as shown in the figure below.

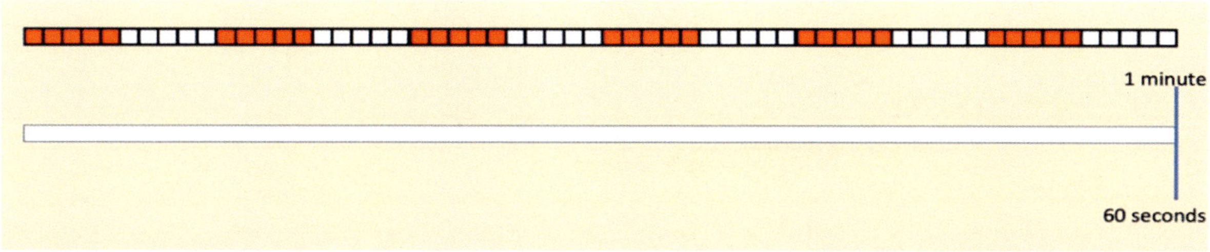

Show one number at a time from the string of related problems below and ask students to determine where the mark should go, each time justifying their reasoning. When consensus is reached make the mark on the bar and mark the seconds underneath. Invite discussion on how much of a minute has passed. The adding machine paper is used so that you can fold the strip in half, to show that 30 seconds is half of a minute and in fourths to show how 15 seconds is a fourth of a minute and that a minute can be divided into four fourths of 15 seconds each.

The String

30

15

45

E8: Time

This string is like E7 except that it focuses on 60 minutes and 1 hour instead of 60 seconds and 1 minute. String an alternating length of 60 connecting cubes (5 red, 5 white, 5 red, 5 white, etc.) along a white board. Draw a line beneath the cubes, but this time at the end write 60 minutes. Explain that time can be measured in hours and that 60 minutes is one hour long. Mark one hour at the top of the line.

Show one number at a time from the string of related problems and ask students to determine where the mark should go, each time justifying their reasoning. When consensus is reached make the mark on the bar and mark the minutes underneath. This string gets students to think about the half hour as 30 minutes, and then has them thinking about 5-minute intervals – 5 minutes before an hour is 55 and 5 minutes before a half hour is 25, 5 minutes after the half hour is 35 minutes. This is not a year-end objective for grade one but will be a nice challenge. Approach it as fun.

The String

30

5

15

55

25

35

E9: Time

This string is like E7.

The String

30

10

20

40

50

E10: Clock Images

These strings use clock images to focus on telling time by the hour and half hour. On P2S2: a personalized professional support system (NPO's online platform), in the unit *The Timekeepers*, there is an interactive clock within the online resources. You can also use a MathRack™ clock (available at www.mathrack.com), which has movable hands and shows five-minute increments with alternating red and white beads.

Show images on the analog clock (one-at-a-time) of the times listed below in the string, each time asking, *"What time is it?"* Invite discussion and once everyone agrees with the time, write it in a digital version. Also use the language in the string (for example writing and saying 2:30 but also saying half-past two). As you move from one image to another in the string, invite students to talk about what the hands have done. For example, to get to 4:00 from 3:30, the minute hand moved 30 minutes – a half-hour more.

The String

Two o'clock (2:00)

Half-past two (2:30)

Three o'clock (3:00)

Half-past three (3:30)

Four o'clock (4:00)

Half-past four (4:30)

E11: Clock Images

This string is similar to E10.

The String

Twelve o'clock (12:00)

Half-past twelve (12:30)

One o'clock (1:00)

Three o'clock (3:00)

Half-past three (3:30)

Half-past four (4:30)

Half-past five (5:30)

Six o'clock (6:00)

Behind the Numbers

The times have been chosen carefully to support students to consider, not just what the clock says, but to also consider the duration of the time change. The duration of elapsed time from 12:00 to 12:30 is 30 minutes or half an hour. Providing the images consecutively supports students to understand why 12:30 can also be referred to as half past two. By doing 1:00 next, students are challenged to consider how the other half of an hour completes a full turn of the minute hand, but also why on a clock 1 comes next and not 13. This is an opportunity to explain that there are twelve numbers on a clock and that midnight is 12 AM and noon is 12 PM.

E12: Clock Images

This string is like E10.

The String

Nine o'clock (9:00)

Half-past nine (9:30)

Ten o'clock (10:00)

Half-past ten (10:30)

Half-past eleven (11:30)

Half-past twelve (12:30)

One o'clock (1:00)

E13: Clock Images

This string is like E10.

The String

Six o'clock (6:00)

Half-past six (6:30)

Seven o'clock (7:00)

Half-past seven (7:30)

Half-past eight (8:30)

Nine o'clock (9:00)

Appendix A – Images for String D7 (1 of 3)

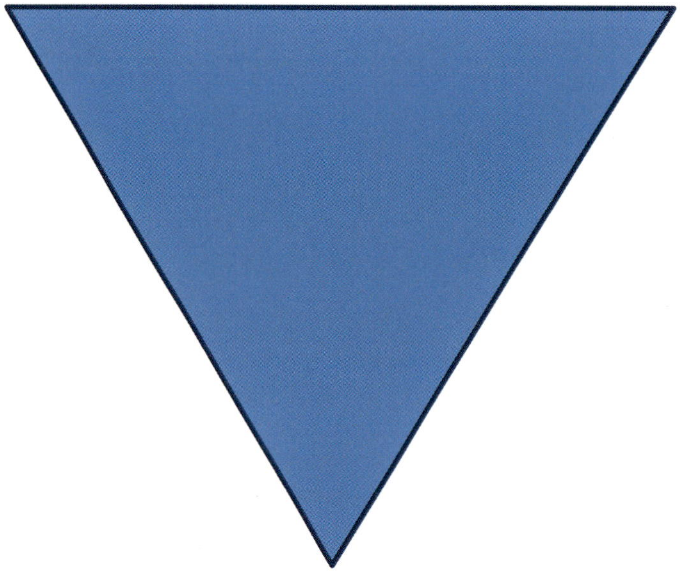

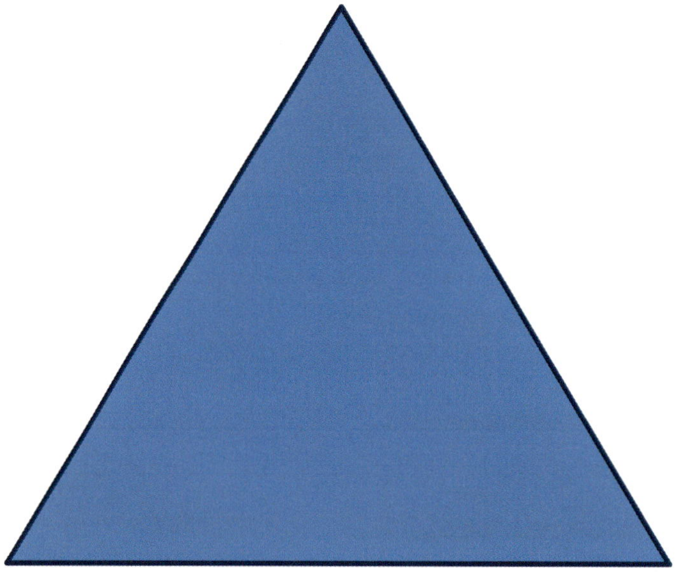

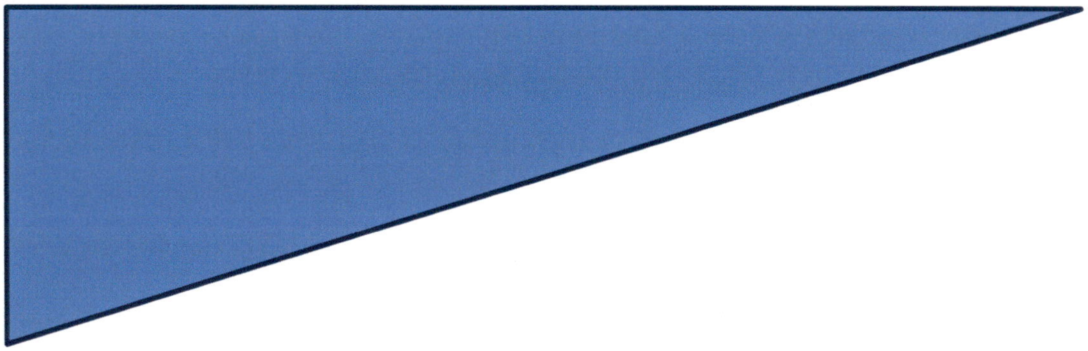

Appendix A – Images for String D7 (3 of 3)

Appendix B – Images for String D8 (1 of 3)

Appendix C – Images for String D9 (1 of 3)

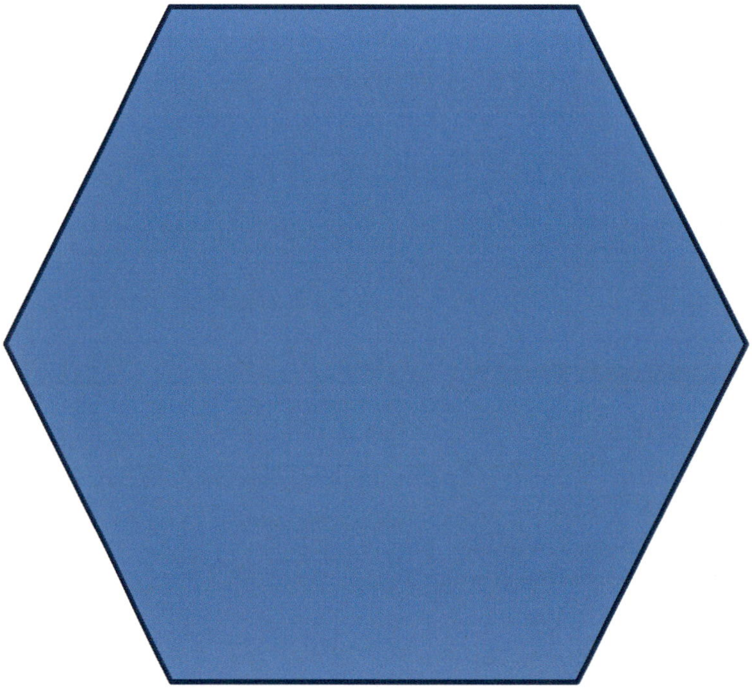

Appendix C – Images for String D9 (2 of 3)

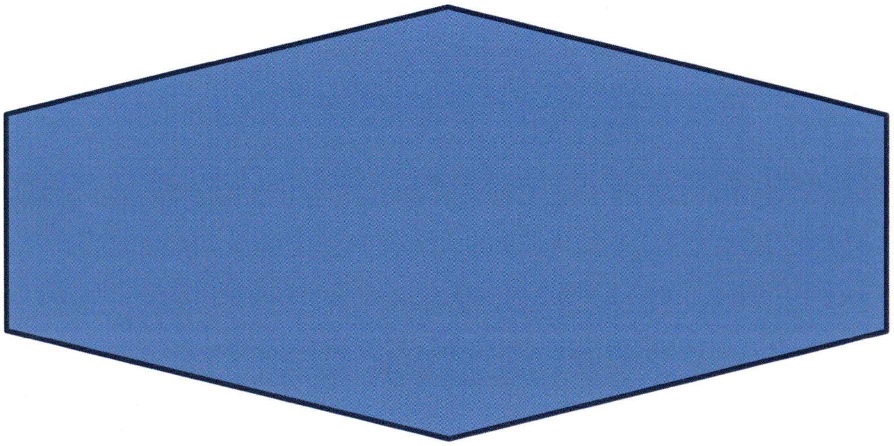

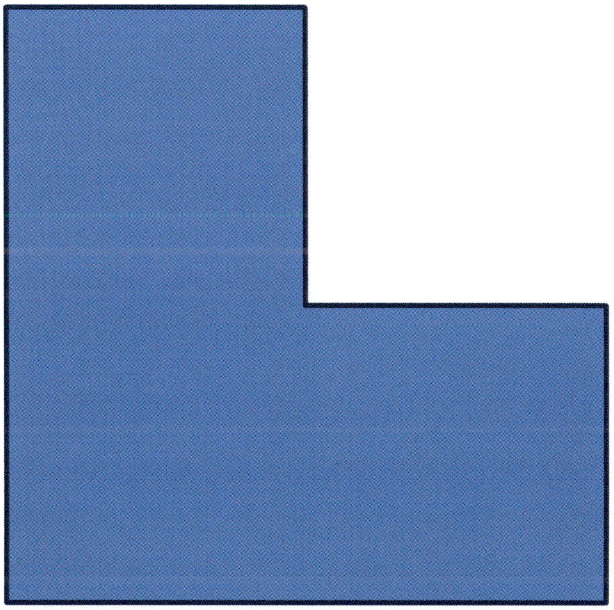

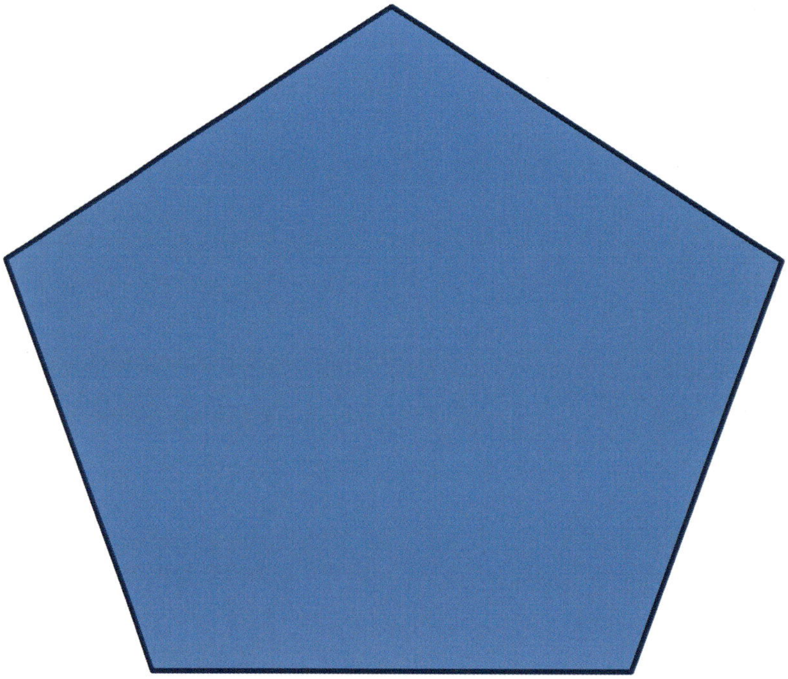

Appendix D – Images for String D10 (1 of 3)

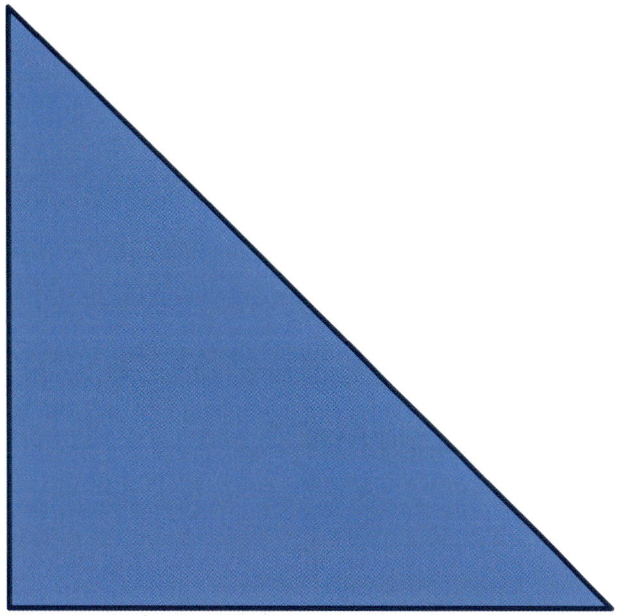

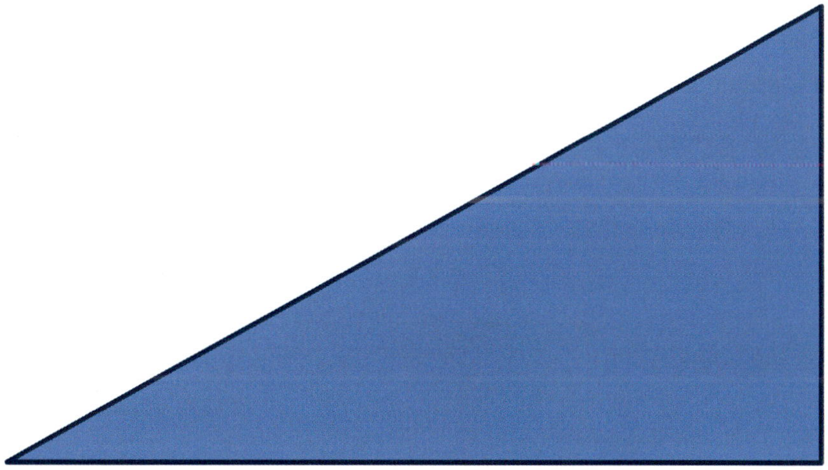

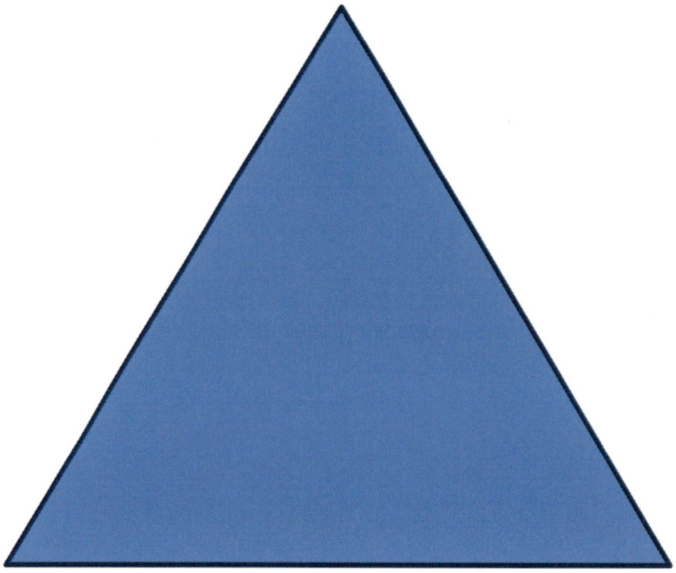

Appendix D – Images for String D10 (3 of 3)

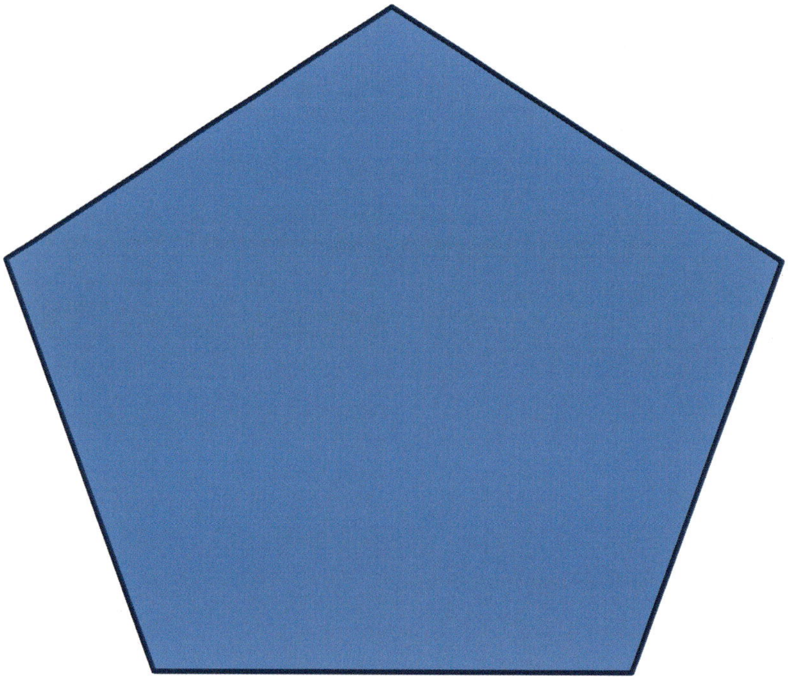

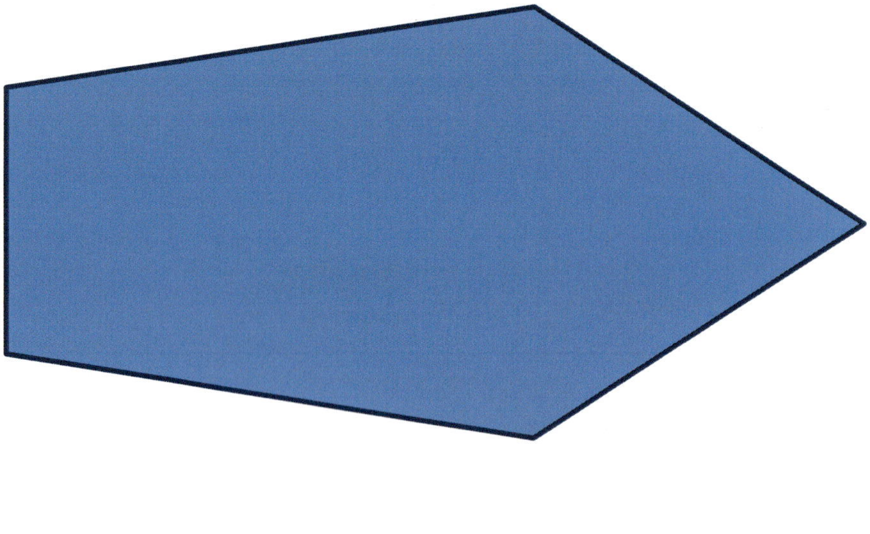

Appendix E – Images for String D11 (2 of 3)

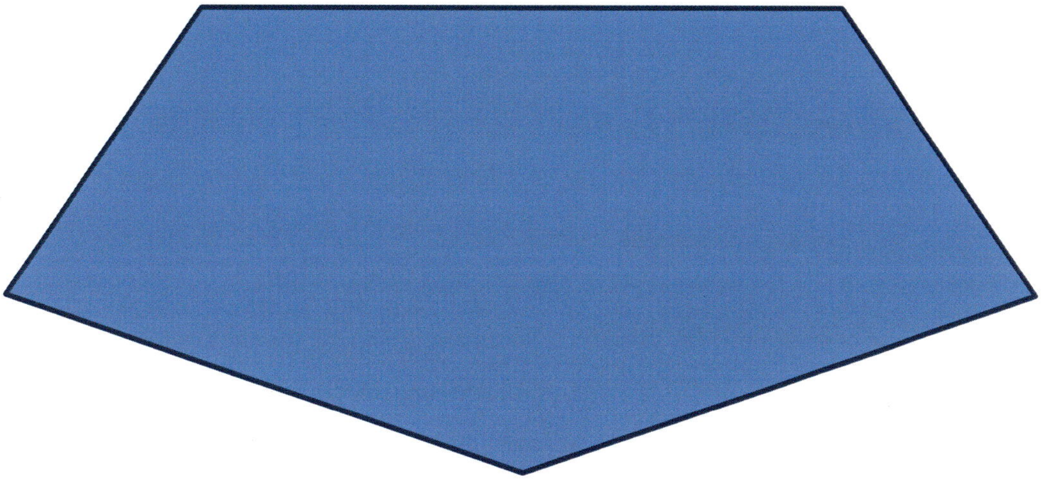

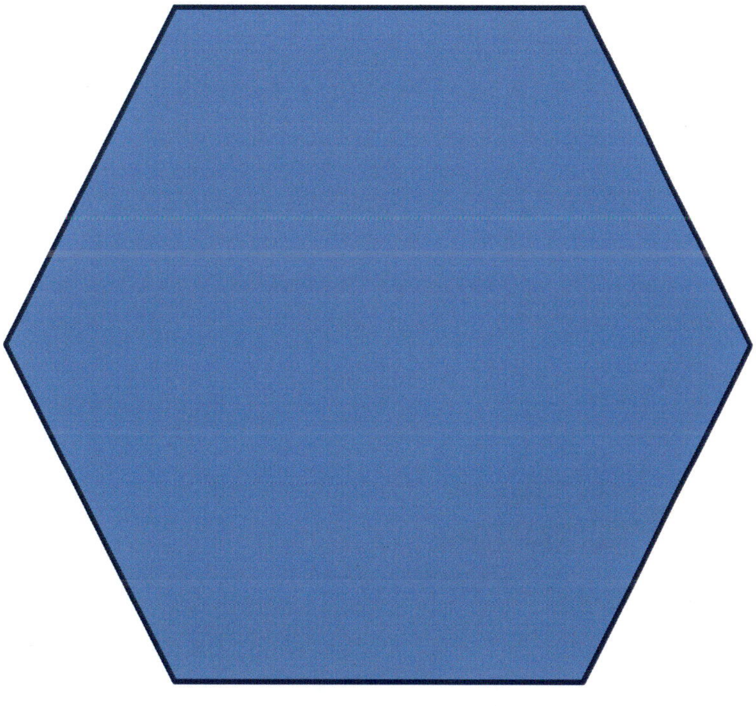

Appendix E – Images for String D11 (3 of 3)

Appendix F – Images for String D12

Appendix G – Images for String D13 (1 of 3)

Appendix G – Images for String D13 (2 of 3)

Appendix H – Images for String D14 (1 of 2)

Appendix H – Images for String D14 (2 of 2)

Appendix I – Images for String D15 (1 of 2)

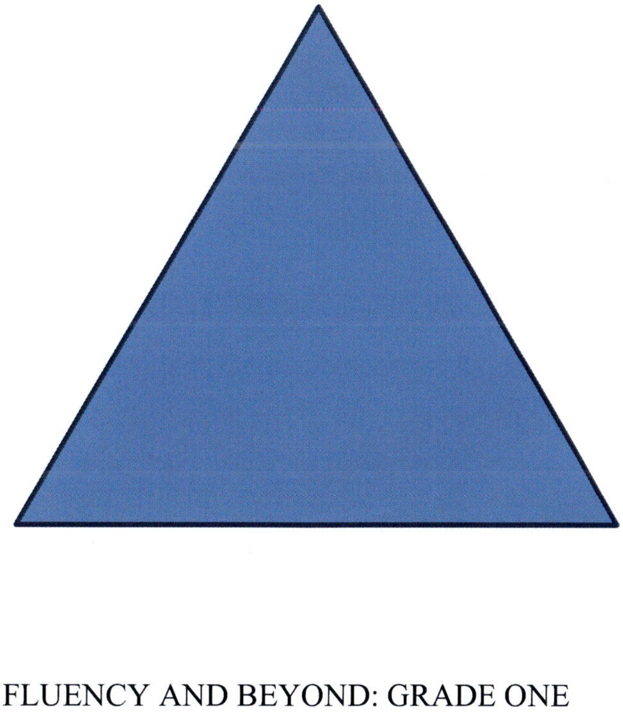

Appendix I – Images for String D15 (2 of 2)

Appendix J – Images for String D16 (1 of 2)

Appendix J – Images for String D16 (2 of 2)

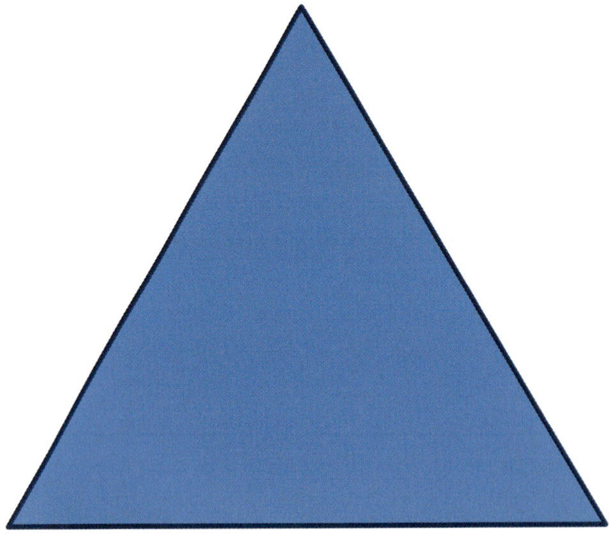

Appendix K – Image for String D17

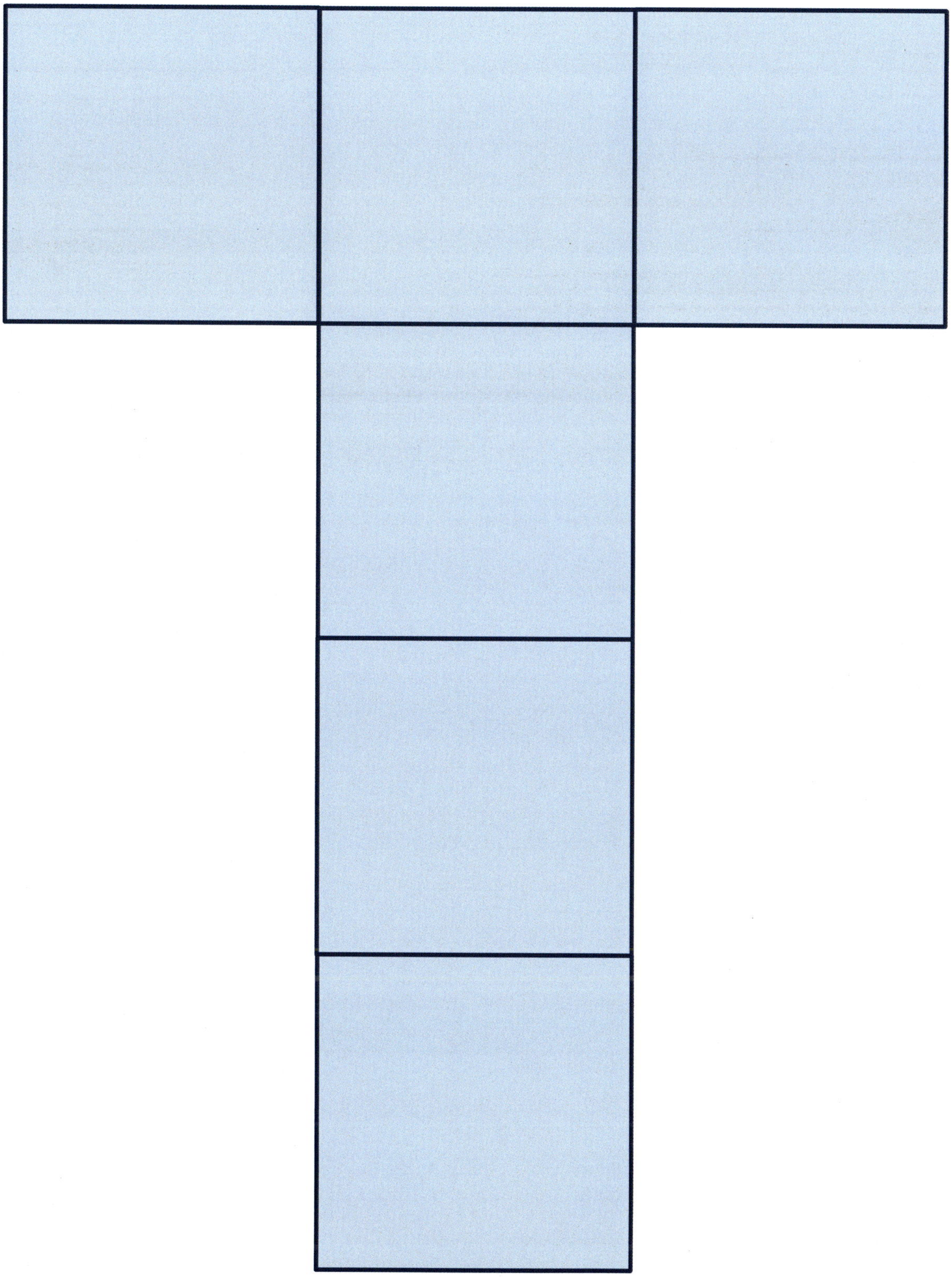

Appendix L – Image for String D18

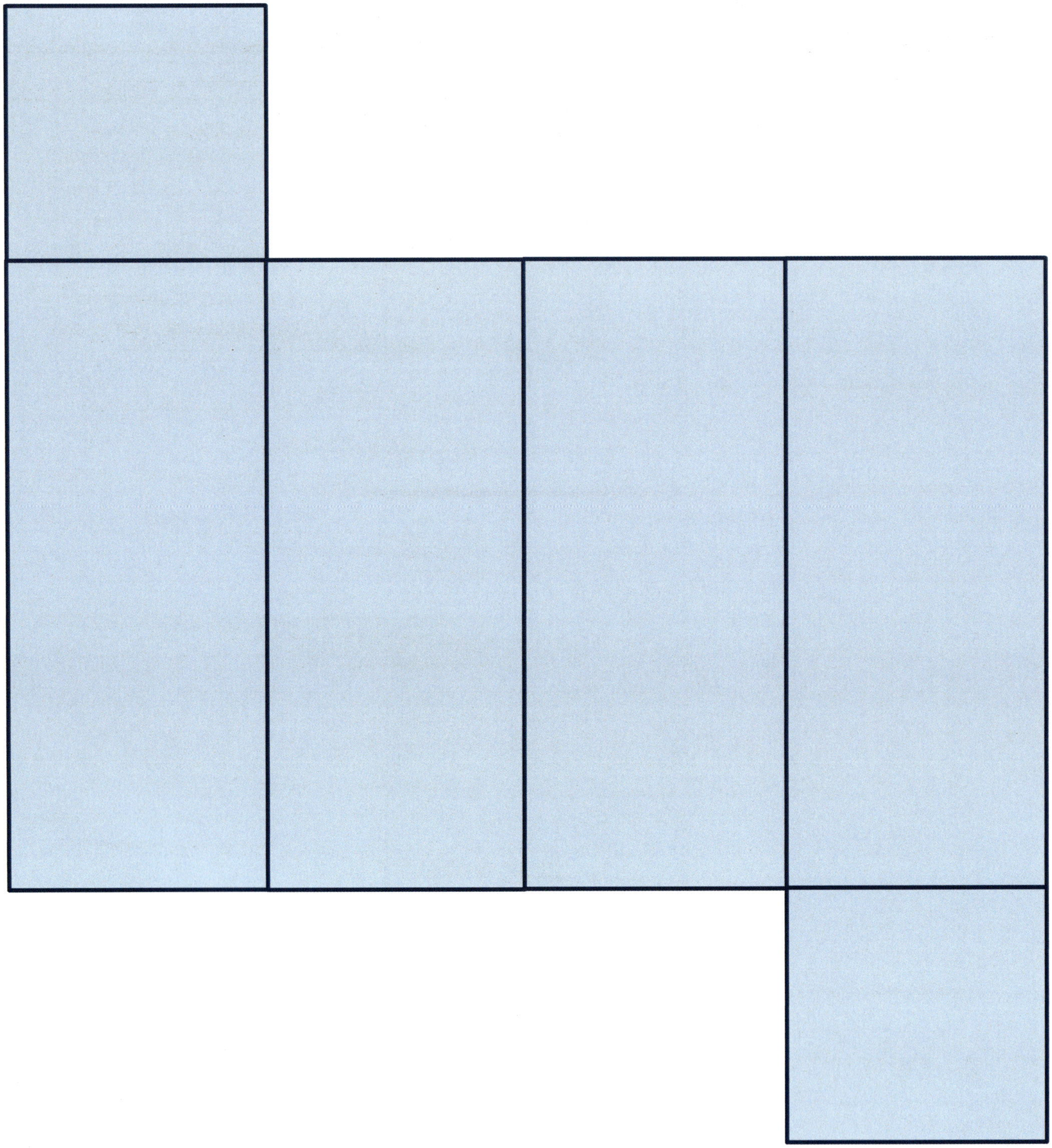

Appendix M – Image for String D19

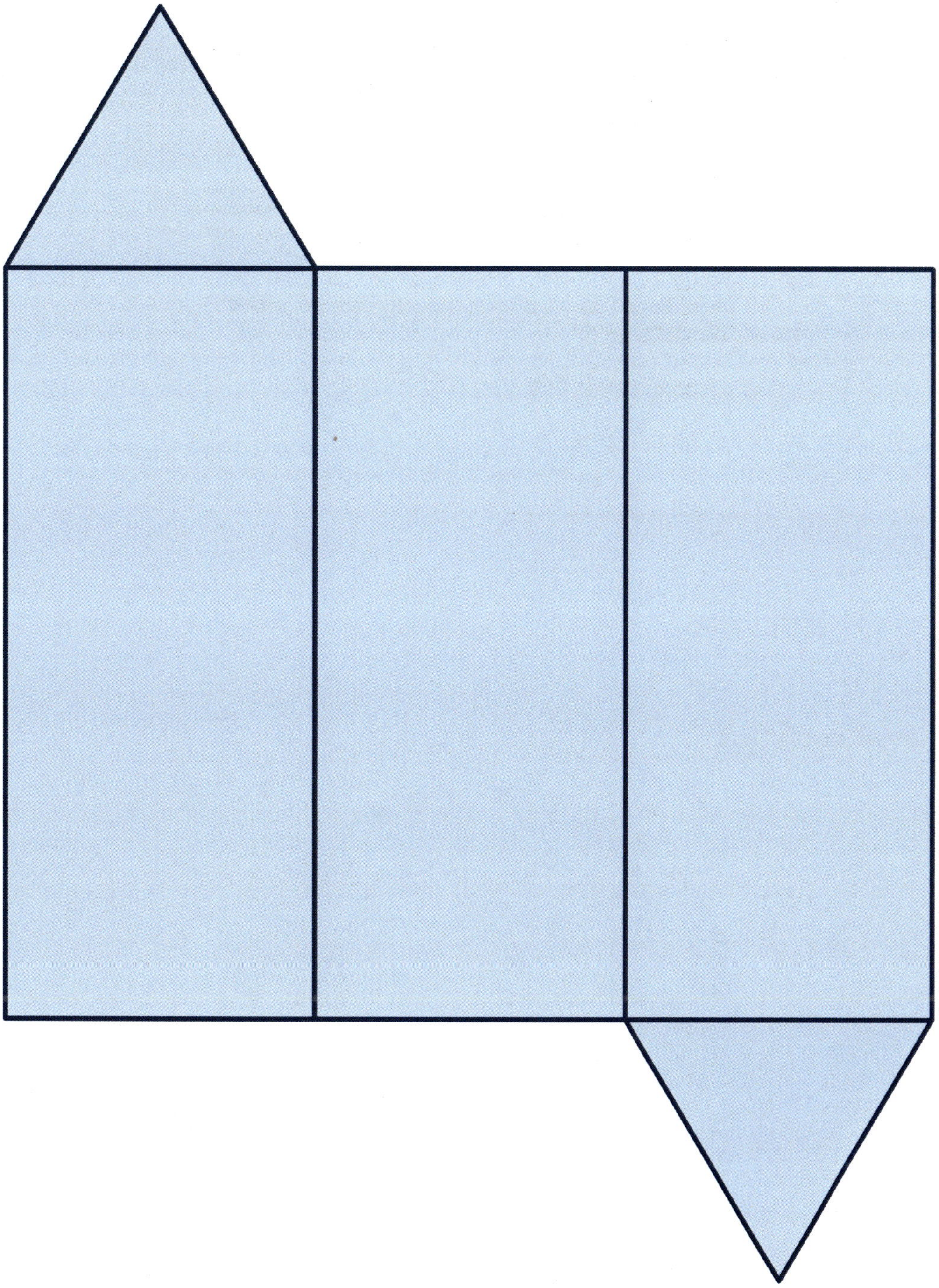

Appendix N – Images for String D20 (1 of 3)

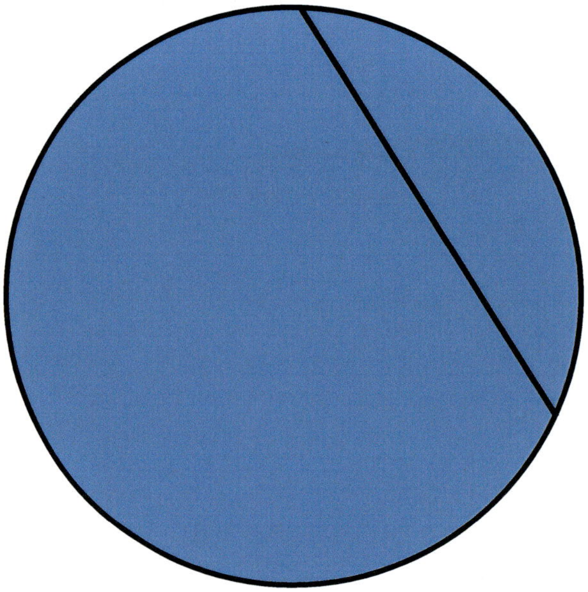

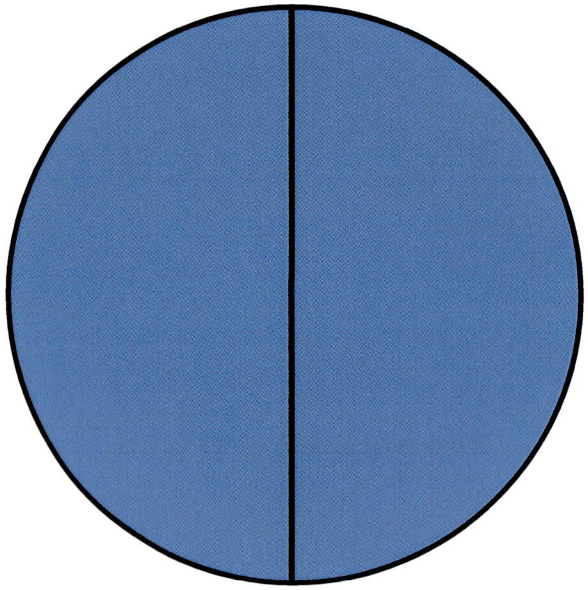

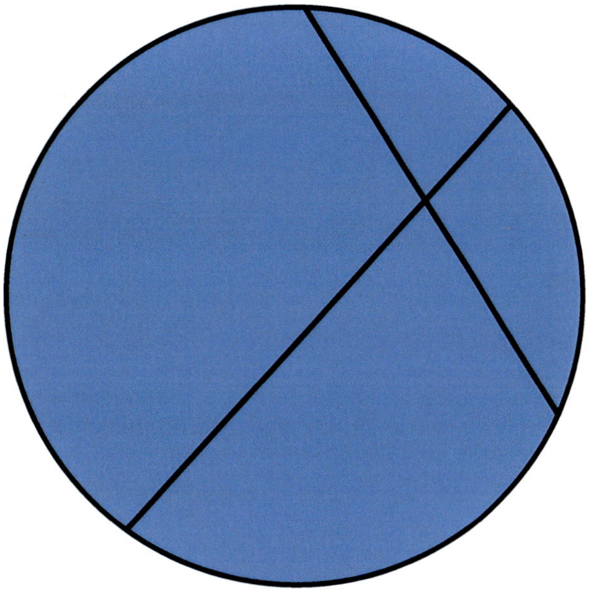

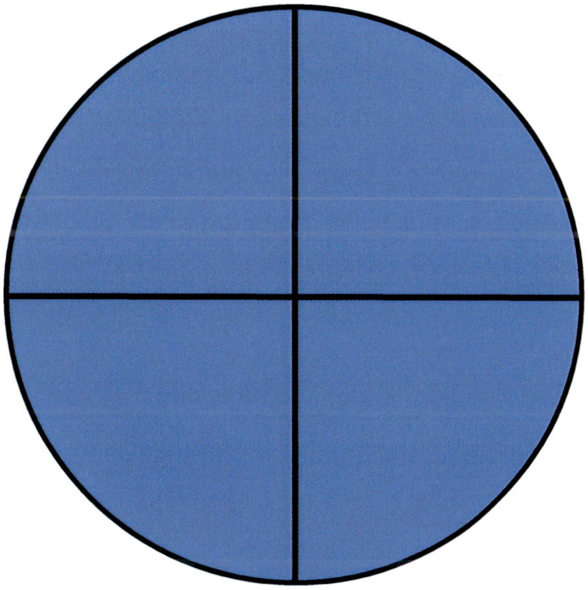

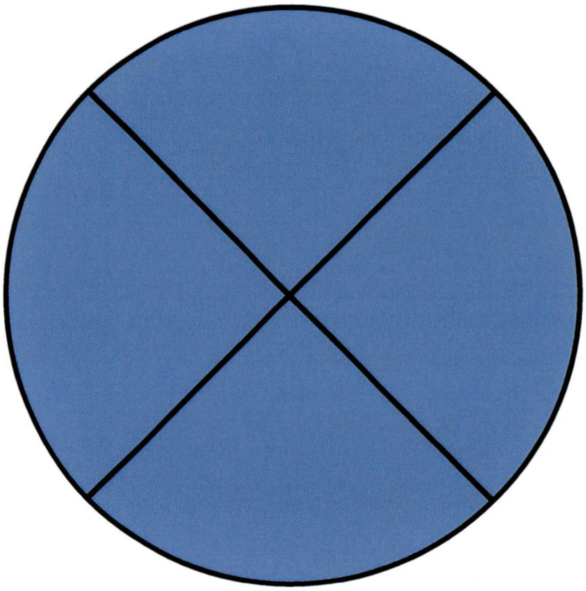

Appendix O – Images for String D21 (1 of 3)

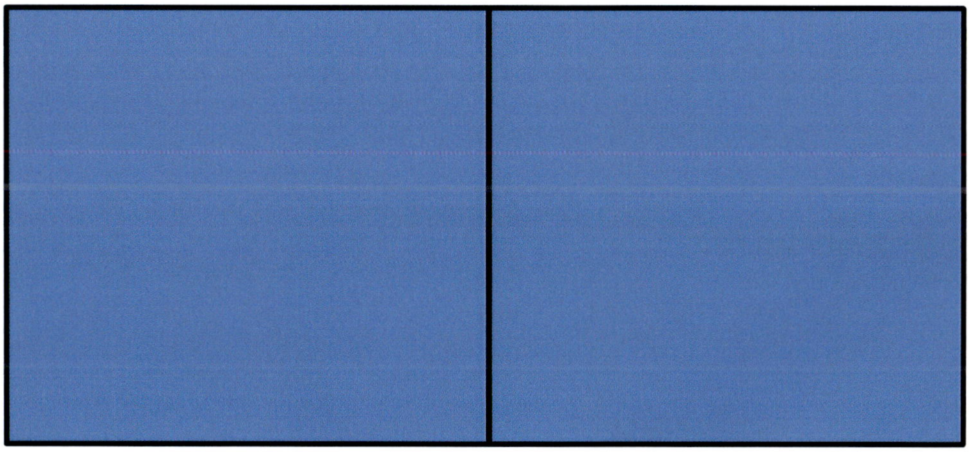

Appendix O – Images for String D21 (2 of 3)

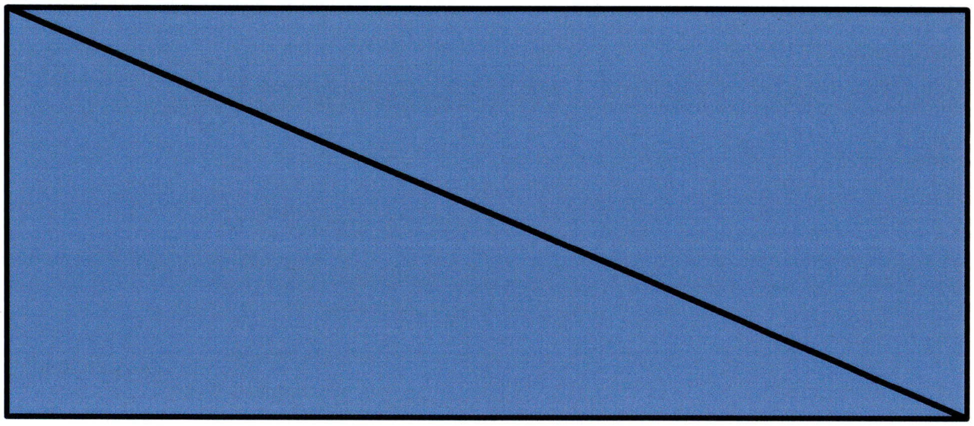

Appendix P – Images for String D22 (1 of 2)

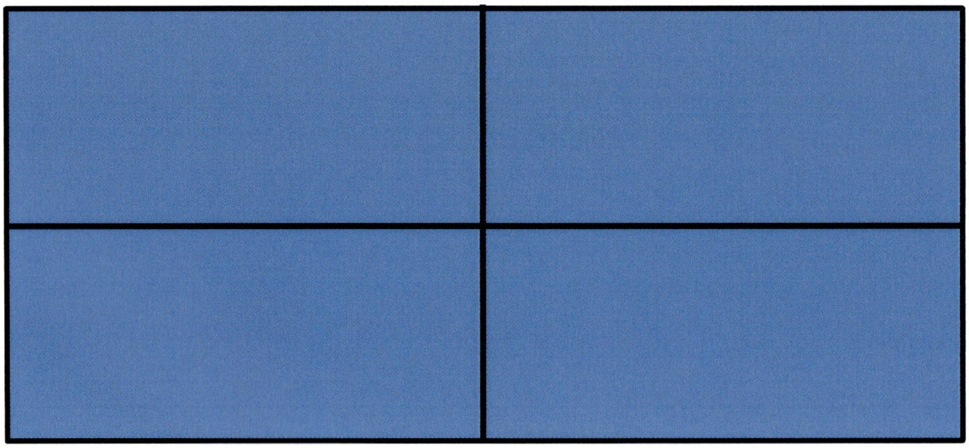

Appendix P – Images for String D22 (2 of 2)

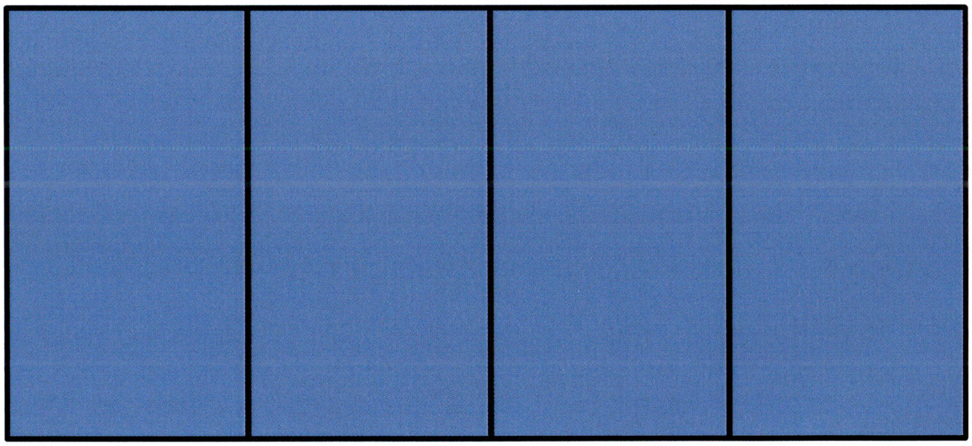

Appendix Q – Images for String D23 (1 of 2)

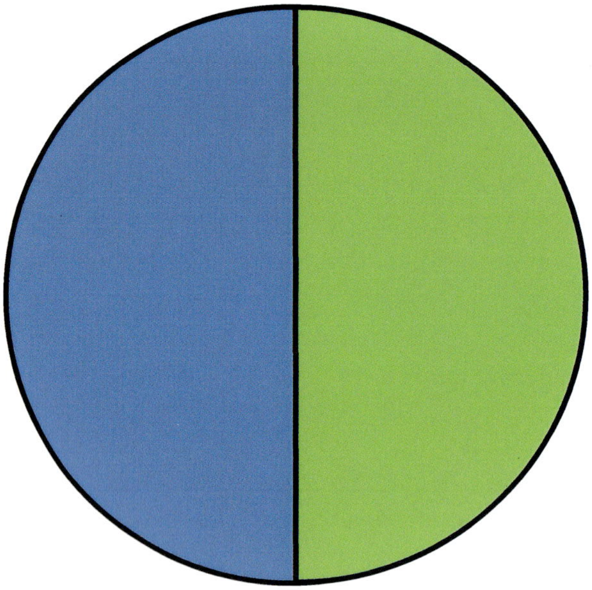

Appendix Q – Images for String D22 (2 of 2)

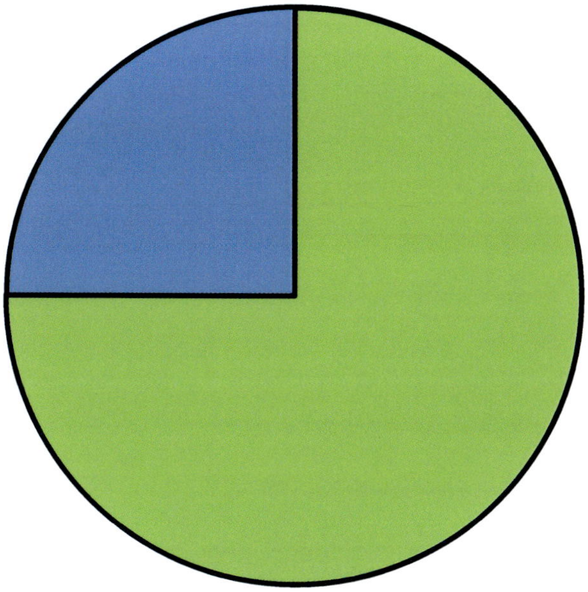

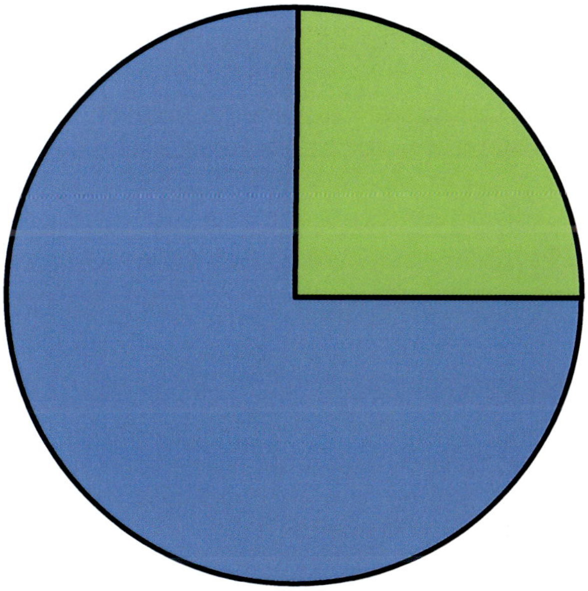

Made in the USA
Coppell, TX
21 June 2026

83197769R00090